# HEARTS,
# HEADS,
# & HANDS

# MODULE

3

# HEARTS,
# HEADS,
# & HANDS

*Worship*
*Christian Doctrine*
*Shepherding God's Flock*

# M. DAVID SILLS

PUBLISHING GROUP
NASHVILLE, TENNESSEE

978-1-4336-4693-5

Published by B&H Publishing Group
Nashville, Tennessee

Dewey Decimal Classification: 371.3
Subject Heading: TEACHING \ CHRISTIAN
MISSIONARIES—TRAINING \ MISSIONS—
STUDY AND TEACHING

1 2 3 4 5 6 7 8 • 21 20 19 18 17

# Dedication

While my travels, reading, research, and ministry of reaching, preaching, and teaching throughout the world and throughout the years have repeatedly demonstrated to me the great need for a contextualizable training program—one that is not simply a Western education translated and force fed to pastors and leaders around the world—it was the highland Quichuas of Ecuador who first showed me the need for such a model. They were also the first to have it field tested among them, which made it possible to tweak and contour the content and method, and make countless improvements and additions along the way. These brothers and sisters patiently helped me to understand what they needed to learn and the way they needed to learn it, which opened my eyes to the global need for pastoral and leadership training that is both culturally appropriate and biblically faithful.

This training is dedicated to all the men and women around the world who strive to serve God and His church in the ministries He has given them while burdened by their lack of knowledge and inability to get the training they know they need. More specifically, this is dedicated to the Quichua people who are so dear to me—to the pastors, leaders, and churches that are as well as to those that are yet to be.

May they be found faithful, and may this resource be a tool that helps them be so.

# Acknowledgments

Books are not conceived and published by one person alone. Entire teams of dedicated and hard-working people collaborate, whether consciously or not, in a process that culminates in the books you see lining the shelves of libraries and bookstores. Few books have owed as much to others as the *Hearts, Heads, and Hands* training material, including the module you hold in your hands. This training material is different from the other books I have written. It covers areas beyond my normal research and teaching, running throughout the breadth of the theological encyclopedia and all the preparation that is necessary for Christian leadership. As such, this resource is the result of what I have read and learned all my Christian life. All those who have played some role in making me who I am have fed into this stream that now empties into the ocean, that will in turn influence all the shores it touches. The teaching and examples of my parents, family, and both the pastors and members of the Baptist churches of my upbringing and ministry are distilled into these pages. All of my friends and experiences are threads of the tapestry of my life, and now this book. The instruction and example of my college and seminary professors echo in my mind any time I preach, teach, and write but perhaps never so much as in the writing of this book. Thank you Wynn Kenyon, Dan Fredericks, Jack Glaze, Bill Warren, Sam Larsen, Paul Long, and Elias Medeiros. Thank you especially, Tom Nettles, for your faithful example, teaching, counsel, preaching, and friendship from the day you baptized Mary and me to this day.

I could never have imagined how much creative energy, hard work, and expertise that LifeWay could and would pour into the *Hearts, Heads, and Hands* training material. I am grateful especially to Jennifer Lyell for her tireless efforts, missions vision, and bringing all the necessary LifeWay teams to the table. While it would be impossible to name everyone at LifeWay who has worked to see this effort through and improve it along the way, I want to say a special thank-you to Jennifer, Craig, Cris, and Kim. This could not have been produced without you and the rest of the amazing LifeWay team.

I am profoundly thankful for the leadership of The Southern Baptist Theological Seminary. Drs. R. Albert Mohler, Randy Stinson, and Adam Greenway and our trustees not only very graciously granted me a yearlong sabbatical to free me for researching and writing this content, Southern Seminary has always encouraged me to research, write, and travel for missions throughout my thirteen years as a professor. Many thanks also to Fred and Patty Boeninger for providing "The Best Place" for a writing retreat on Lookout Mountain.

I called on others for insights as I launched into the organization of the content. Thanks to Hannah Carter, Michael Haykin, Tom Nettles, and Steve Weaver. I am deeply grateful for those who reviewed portions of the completed manuscript to critique, correct, and offer suggestions to improve it. Many thanks to Steve Bond for reviewing the Old Testament portions, Brian Vickers on the New Testament, Devin Maddox on Christian doctrine, Rob Plummer on hermeneutics, and Tom Nettles on church history. Their work makes this content much better than it would have been. Please note: the faults that remain are mine alone.

Many thanks also to the staff and missionaries of Reaching & Teaching International Ministries. The need and vision for this book grew out of the actual experience of teaching pastors. My leadership responsibilities with Reaching & Teaching have been ably shouldered by Jon Deedrick and Jason Wright to give me the freedom to focus on writing over the last year and a half.

This training material is longer and its subject area is broader than anything I have written before, and so it required much more of me for a much longer time. Thank you Mary for your patience, support, and encouragement all along the way. Thank you, Christopher, Carol, Molly, and Daniel, for your love and support—and for not letting my grandchildren forget who I was while I was away in the writing cave. Abraham, Anna Liz, Emma, Mary Elle, Naomi, and Claire, Papi's back now. Thank you for waiting!

# Contents

Introduction ............................................................. 1

Module 3 Learning Objectives ............................ 17

Worship, Peace, Just
Christian Doctrine
Shepherding God's Flock ........................................ 21

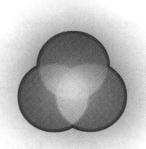

# Introduction

The greatest need in the world today is to preach the gospel to the lost, deeply disciple believers, train leaders, and educate pastors. I do not say this because that is the sum total of the task of Christian ministry, but because these are each equally essential elements of what Christ commanded us to do, and so few are involved in the training aspect of this task as compared to evangelism to reach the unreached. Certainly we must reach the unreached, but we must also fully obey the Great Commission and teach them to observe all that Christ commanded. The missionaries, mission agencies, and national workers who focus on evangelism and reaching the unreached are winning to Christ millions of believers who then need discipleship and training before the missions task can be complete. Because so many missionaries are focusing on reaching the unreached, they often must leave evangelized fields too quickly, resulting in untrained leadership, unintended syncretism, and heresy in churches. Taking into account all that the Bible commands about discipleship and training, and how imbalanced the focus has become, the great tragedy of the world is not that it is unreached but that it is undiscipled.

# Read This First!

## *The Importance*

The fact that you are reading this book reveals that to some degree you agree that pastoral and leadership training is important. We will see that not only is it important, it is essential. God blesses those who commit themselves to glorify Him through lives that live and teach the truth. You will remember the life of Ezra, the priest and scribe during the Babylonian exile. The Bible teaches us that he had the hand of God on him, which resulted in the king granting his requests (7:6) as well as safe passage from Babylon to Jerusalem (7:9; 8:31). The reason he enjoyed this great blessing is stated in 7:10, "Now Ezra had determined in his heart to study the law of the LORD, obey it, and teach its statutes and ordinances in Israel." God is pleased when His servants know His Word, practice it, and teach it to others. But such knowledge is not common, automatic, or possible in a fallen world that is saturated with false worldviews, religions, and worship apart from intentional discipleship of believers and teaching teachers to be able to teach others.

The teaching in the churches around the world, even in evangelical churches, is mixed with error and vestiges of former religions. Pastors are called to correct false beliefs and teaching (2 Tim. 4:2) and maintain biblical fidelity.

The two essential and primary roles of a pastor are to teach truth and to live a life that practices truth. False views of God and false doctrine will always exist where there is no true view of God and sound teaching. The only source of explicit, authoritative truth about God is what He has revealed to us in His Word. Paul wrote that some key responsibilities of a pastor are to teach truth, to maintain a doctrinally pure church, correct those in error, rebuke those who teach heresy, and set an example for the flock.

Command and teach these things. (1 Tim. 4:11)

Pay close attention to your life and your teaching; persevere in these things, for by doing this you will save both yourself and your hearers. (1 Tim. 4:16)

Don't be too quick to appoint anyone as an elder. (1 Tim. 5:22)

And what you have heard from me in the presence of many witnesses, commit to faithful men who will be able to teach others also. (2 Tim. 2:2)

All Scripture is inspired by God and is profitable
for teaching, for rebuking, for correcting, for
training in righteousness, so that the man of God
may be complete, equipped for every good work.
(2 Tim. 3:16–17)

We proclaim Him, warning everyone with all
wisdom, so that we may present everyone mature
in Christ. (Col. 1:28)

But you must say the things that are consistent
with sound teaching. (Titus 2:1)

A man of grace should be a gracious man. A pastor
must model this characteristic and not be a demanding,
harsh taskmaster who holds his people to impossible standards that he himself is not able to attain. Churches around
the world sometimes suffer spiritual abuse and manipulation by men who base their power in their positions. Many
seminaries, divinity schools, and pastoral training institu-
tions graduate new church leaders with huge heads but little
hearts. In the absence of intentional integral preparation,
men often go into churches with full heads but carnal leadership, politics, and intimidation, and are guilty of ministry
malpractice. The goal of this curriculum is to prepare the
whole person—head, hearts, and hands. We are to focus on
the whole disciple, training to have minds for God, hearts
for truth, and hands that are skilled for the task.

Practically speaking, the best pastor is one whose life is modeled after Christ's and whose teaching flows from His Word. Paul delineated the requirements for pastors in 1 Timothy 3:1–7. In verse 2, Paul says that the pastor must be an able teacher, and to be apt to teach, one must know *what* to teach. In Titus 1:5–9, Paul gives a parallel listing of pastoral requirements. In verse 9, Paul wrote that the pastor must be "holding to the faithful message as taught, so that he will be able both to encourage with sound teaching and to refute those who contradict it." This requires full-orbed ministerial formation because, as James wrote, "Not many should become teachers, my brothers, knowing that we will receive a stricter judgment" (James 3:1).

The pastor is not to do all the work of the ministry in a local church as if he were a hired hand to do all that is necessary; he is to prepare God's people so that *they* can do the work of the church.

And He personally gave some to be apostles,
some prophets, some evangelists, some pastors
and teachers, for the training of the saints in the
work of ministry, to build up the body of Christ,
until we all reach unity in the faith and in the
knowledge of God's Son, growing into a mature
man with a stature measured by Christ's fullness.
Then we will no longer be little children, tossed
by the waves and blown around by every wind of

teaching, by human cunning with cleverness in the
techniques of deceit. (Eph. 4:11–14)

Sound doctrine and biblically faithful teaching are
foundational for shepherding their flock. Peter wrote in
1 Peter 5:1–3, "Therefore, as a fellow elder and witness
to the sufferings of the Messiah and also a participant in
the glory about to be revealed, I exhort the elders among
you: Shepherd God's flock among you, not overseeing out
of compulsion but freely, according to God's will; not for
the money but eagerly; not lording it over those entrusted
to you, but being examples to the flock." Being an example is a crucial part of the work of a pastor. But how can
he model that which he has never learned or embraced.
Knowing, doing, and saying are the three essential aspects
of pastoral ministry.

This saying is trustworthy: "If anyone aspires
to be an overseer, he desires a noble work." An
overseer, therefore, must be **above reproach,** the
**husband of one wife, self-controlled, sensible,**
**respectable, hospitable, an able teacher, not**
**addicted to wine, not a bully but gentle, not**
**quarrelsome, not greedy**—one who **manages his**
**own household competently, having his children**
**under control with all dignity.** (If anyone does not
know how to manage his own household, how
will he take care of God's church?) He must **not**
**be a new convert,** or he might become conceited

and fall into the condemnation of the Devil. Furthermore, he must have a **good reputation among outsiders,** so that he does not fall into disgrace and the Devil's trap. (1 Tim. 3:1–7, emphasis mine)

The reason I left you in Crete was to set right what was left undone and, as I directed you, to appoint elders in every town: one who is **blameless, the husband of one wife, having faithful children not accused of wildness or rebellion.** For an overseer, as God's administrator, must be **blameless, not arrogant, not hot-tempered, not addicted to wine, not a bully, not greedy for money, but hospitable, loving what is good, sensible, righteous, holy, self-controlled, holding to the faithful message as taught,** so that he will be able both to encourage with sound teaching and to refute those who contradict it. (Titus 1:5–9, emphasis mine)

These required qualifications are not mysterious, but rather very clear descriptions. They are not good ideas or superfluous guidelines for more developed churches; they are basic requirements and should be commonly found. To the degree that we place pastors over churches without consideration of the biblical qualifications for pastors, we set churches up for heartache and error.

## The Needs

There is an overwhelming need for trained pastors to
interpret and teach God's Word faithfully to His people
around the world. It is estimated that although many
churches do not have pastors, and many pastors must of
necessity serve more than one church in the regions where
they live, an estimated 85 percent of the pastors around the
world have no theological education or pastoral training.[1]
While it would be comparatively easy to simply translate
and hand out the books used for Western education pro-
grams, the majority of the world cannot read well enough
to learn new information that way. Only about one of
every five persons in the world could pick up a book they
have not seen, read it while following the author's thesis
and argument, reflect on what was read, and write a short
response. Yet, over 90 percent of all our tools for evangelism, discipleship, and leadership training has been produced for highly literate people.[2] Pastoral training models

---

[1] The source for this statistic is unknown, although it is a
widely accepted statistic illustrating that experience and observa-
tion by multiple organizations and individuals have found it to be
consistent with anecdotes and observations. Organizations that
have cited this statistic include The Gospel Coalition, Training
Leaders International, Equipping the Church International, and
Leadership Resources.

[2] Durk Meijer, "Third International Orality Conference: His
Word Must Go Beyond the Printed Page to Oral Media," http://
www.lausanneworldpulse.com/perspectives.php/20/09-2005.

must consider the reading abilities and learning styles of the world's cultures.

As new believers grapple to practice their faith, the absence of discipleship and training is painfully obvious to them, if not to the missionaries who evangelize them. We sometimes think that a new believer with the Spirit and a Bible needs nothing else; after all, the Spirit will guide him into all truth. Aside from being a mistaken interpretation of John 16:13, that notion overlooks all of the biblical commands to disciple and teach those who come behind us. People do not remain in a knowledge vacuum; they will fill in the unknown gaps with what seems correct to them, borrowing from the traditions of the past and adding in the little they know of Christianity, thus creating syncretism and teaching false doctrine.

## *Reaching and Teaching Pastoral Training Model*

The model for this *Hearts, Heads, and Hands* theological education, leadership training, and pastoral preparation program grew out of the need to train pastors and disciples around the world, and to train them to train others. Reaching & Teaching International Ministries has used this model for training with great effectiveness in multiple countries and among leaders of all levels of educational background.

We train hearts, heads, and hands in an integrated fashion, constantly connecting personal discipleship to the content of traditional theological education and teaching

practical pastoral ministry applications. We begin each
module with a personal spiritual discipline, explain what it
is, how to practice it, and why it's important, and then we
actually model it. We then move into the head knowledge
instruction, which more closely resembles what you would
expect in pastoral education. Each module ends with the
hands portion, which is training in the skill set for leading
others and pastoral ministry, including practical aspects of
mentoring leaders, managing church finances, administra-
tion, etc.

We challenge you to pour into the lives of others
what you learn in this program as a step in fulfillment of
2 Timothy 2:2. As you do so, you will find that teaching
others grants several additional benefits. Teaching another
person enables you to cement the lesson into other parts of
your brain and memory. It also helps you to think about
the material from other aspects as your students ask questions you had not considered. You discover what you had
not actually learned as well as you thought. Finally, and
perhaps most importantly, the practice of teaching others
teaches you how to teach. In the process of teaching others you learn how to communicate truth, where you need
to improve, and the joy of seeing your own students learn
and embrace truth. Of course, you should encourage your
own students to teach others also so that the principle of
multiplication will continue.

The goal of Christian ministers is to evangelize, disciple, and teach others to do the same. You want to be

and prepare disciples who are more than merely success-
ful graduates of an academic program. Churches require
godly, well-trained pastors and leaders with hearts for
God, heads filled with truth, and hands that are skilled
to minister. The way forward is training the whole person
with the whole truth for the whole ministry.

These chapters are not intended to be an in-depth, academic treatment of subjects, nor do they claim to offer new
insights or refutations to contemporary scholarly works.
These chapters are not written for the scholarly academy,
but are the components of a deep discipleship or pastoral
training program. My only "right" qualification, or even
audacity, to write this book and compile this curriculum is
simply the calling and passion that God has placed on my
life—to see you as pastors and leaders of Christ's global
church thoroughly prepared and equipped for every good
work.

For those of you wishing to go deeper, and for teachers
desiring more background as you prepare to teach, each
chapter will conclude with a short list of suggested reading. Some of you will want and need more than this text
is designed to address, yet you may not have access to a
formal seminary education for any number of reasons.
The short lists of suggested works listed at the end of each
chapter are for going deeper in your study as you have
opportunity. Here is the content of what you will learn
throughout this program.

# The Heart: The Leader's Spiritual Development

## *Personal Spiritual Disciplines*

- Bible Intake
- Prayer
- Worship
- Scripture Memorization
- Serving
- Evangelism
- Stewardship
- Fasting
- Silence and Solitude

## *The Nine Aspects of Galatians 5:22–23—Fullness of Spirit*

- Love
- Joy
- Peace
- Patience
- Kindness
- Goodness
- Faith
- Gentleness
- Self-control

## *The Nine Aspects of Philippians 4:8–9—Thought Life*

- Truth

- Honorable
- Just
- Purity
- Lovely
- Commendable
- Excellence
- Praiseworthy
- Peace

## The Head: The Leader's Biblical Foundation

- Overview of the Old Testament
- Overview of the New Testament
- Christian Doctrine
- Church History
- Hermeneutics
- Missions and Church Planting
- Homiletics and Storying
- Family Ministry and Counseling
- Worship Leadership

## The Hands: The Leader's Administrative Responsibility

- God's Call to Ministry
- The Pastor's Character
- Shepherding God's Flock
- Ordinances
- Developing Leaders
- Mentoring

- Community Engagement
- Church Finances
- Church Discipline

The curriculum includes these integrated building blocks:

- Module 1
    1. Bible Intake, Love, Truth
    2. Overview of the Old Testament
    3. God's Call to Ministry

- Module 2
    1. Prayer, Joy, Honorable
    2. Overview of the New Testament
    3. The Pastor's Character

- Module 3
    1. Worship, Peace, Just
    2. Christian Doctrine
    3. Shepherding God's Flock

- Module 4
    1. Scripture Memorization, Patience, Purity
    2. Church History
    3. Ordinances

- Module 5
    1. Serving, Kindness, Lovely
    2. Hermeneutics
    3. Developing Leaders

- Module 6
    1. Evangelism, Goodness, Commendable
    2. Missions and Church Planting
    3. Mentoring
- Module 7
    1. Stewardship, Faith, Excellence
    2. Homiletics and Storying
    3. Community Engagement
- Module 8
    1. Fasting, Gentleness, Praiseworthy
    2. Family Ministry and Counseling
    3. Church Finances
- Module 9
    1. Silence and Solitude, Self-control, Peace
    2. Worship Leadership
    3. Church Discipline

We proclaim Him, warning and teaching everyone with all wisdom, so that we may present everyone mature in Christ. (Col. 1:28)

And what you have heard from me in the presence of many witnesses, commit to faithful men who will be able to teach others also. (2 Tim. 2:2)

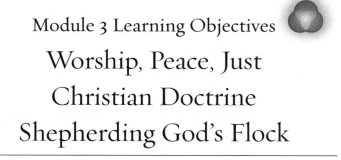

Module 3 Learning Objectives
# Worship, Peace, Just
# Christian Doctrine
# Shepherding God's Flock

At the end of this module, you will be able to:

## 1. The Heart: Worship, Peace, Just

- Describe a personal devotional practice of worship as one's heartfelt expression of love, adoration, honor, veneration, and reverence toward God
- Explain why the Bible is our textbook for worship and the dangers of other guides
- Cite biblical examples of public (corporate) and private (personal) worship in the Old Testament, New Testament—specifically in the life of Jesus—and importance
- Talk about the pastoral importance of developing the fruit of the Spirit, which is peace
- Explain what Paul means about focusing the pastor's thought life on what is just

## 2. The Head: Christian Doctrine

- Explain the differences between and advantages of biblical and systematic theology

- Describe the unique characteristics of Catholic theology and how it differs from evangelical theology
- Describe the unique characteristics of liberation theology and how it differs from evangelical theology
- Explain the following doctrines as understood in evangelical Christian doctrine: Revelation, Nature and Attributes of God, Trinity, Creation, Providence, the Virgin Birth, Humanity and Deity of Jesus Christ, Atonement, Resurrection and Ascension, Christ's Threefold Office of Prophet, Priest and King, Holy Spirit, Humanity and the Fall, Salvation, Election, Regeneration, Conversion, Saving Faith, Repentance, Justification, Adoption, Sanctification, Baptism and Filling of Holy Spirit, Perseverance of the Saints, Death, Intermediate State, Glorification, Church, Eschatology, Millennial Views, Final Judgment, Hell, and Heaven

## 3. The Hands: Shepherding God's Flock

- Explain God's plan for church leadership and who its shepherds should be
- Cite New Testament passages and terms that discuss the roles shepherds fulfill
- Describe what God's Word teaches about the flock, providing metaphors

- Discuss instructive biblical commands, models, and descriptions for understanding what shepherds should guide their churches to be and do
- Explain biblically why evangelicals believe that the flock belongs to Christ

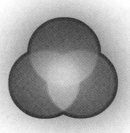

# Worship, Peace, Just
# Christian Doctrine
# Shepherding God's Flock

## The Heart: Worship, Peace, Just

### Overview

Christian leaders must be prepared to lead in worship, be biblically grounded in sound doctrine, and shepherd God's flock as God has instructed. It is often said, "As the pastor goes, so goes the church." A shepherd cannot lead the flock any higher than he himself has gone. It is instructive that the Holy Spirit chose the metaphor of sheep rather than goats to refer to God's people. While goats may be driven, sheep must be led. As the pastor ascends to greater heights in devotion and doctrinal purity, those who follow him may also. The responsibilities of shepherds are commanded, modeled, and informed throughout the Bible.

This module will instruct the heart in worship—not the corporate worship we are familiar with on Sundays, but the worship of God in our devotional time as a personal spiritual discipline. This practice of personal worship of God in a pastor's life will be as obvious to those who are around him as its absence would be. Profound devotion and personal worship shape and change a person for good or ill, depending on the object of worship. Dedicate and prepare yourself to have a heart that desires communion with the one true and living God more than anything else.

As noted in the Old and New Testament overviews, all the cultures of the world already embrace some religion of their own devising, which means that they already worship something. The peoples of the world must hear the truth of the gospel message and come to know the One who is the Truth, the Way, and the Life in order to truly know and worship Him. We noted that the source of the truth that they need is the Bible. Since no one could ascend into heaven to conduct research and then return to teach the rest of us, God revealed Himself to us in His Word. In the Bible we learn what we are to believe about God, what He wants us to be, and what He wants us to do.

Because many cultures around the world are saturated with false traditional religions, it is imperative that new believers receive deep discipleship, and that the leaders among them get pastoral training that includes biblical studies and theological education. Worldviews give explanation to daily events, origins of the universe, and inner workings of reality for the world's peoples. Such lifelong beliefs do not simply evaporate upon praying a prayer to receive Jesus; new believers must be retaught. Discipleship is commanded and modeled in the Bible for a reason. New understandings about God, sin, salvation, and eternal life must be grounded in the Word of God to replace previously held religious beliefs. Since some of you may be studying the Bible for the first time, learning Christian doctrine through systematic theology *and* biblical theology may be a wise approach.

Biblical theology and systematic theology present the same truths, but are organized differently. Biblical theology is incremental and chronological and demonstrates what God has revealed as the Bible is studied book by book, noting historical realities of the time when the doctrines were first given and the emphasis of the writer. Systematic theology essentially takes all that God has revealed everywhere and places this knowledge under headings such as the doctrines of Scripture, God, man, Christ, the Holy Spirit, sin, salvation, and so forth. Biblical theology is not more *biblical* than systematic theology; it primarily refers to the way the truths God has given are presented. Wayne Grudem wrote, "Systematic theology is any study that answers the

question, 'What does the whole Bible teach us today?'
about any given topic."[3]

The practical training of any pastor must include
how to shepherd God's people. Pastors who entered the
ministry in the past would have been much more familiar with the master-apprentice model than contemporary
Westerners. In this model an experienced pastor mentors
a young pastor. Although the young candidate was a committed disciple, had read many books, and passed exami-
nations, they considered that learning the practical skills to
shepherd God's flock through on-the-job training was just
as important.

A pastor is not to imitate models seen among business
leaders, military sergeants, company bosses, social direc-
tors, or popular entertainers; he is to shepherd God's flock
as God's Word instructs him to do. The core essentials for
training hearts, heads, and hands in this module are personal worship, Christian doctrine, and shepherding God's
flock God's way.

John Bunyan's classic allegory entitled *The Pilgrim's
Progress* describes the journey of Christian on his way to
the Celestial City. Bunyan portrays the path that we all
must walk and warns us of dangers we will face along the
way. One goal of each of these student modules is to help
you grow in sanctification and discipleship as you walk

---

[3] Wayne Grudem, *Systematic Theology: An Introduction to
Biblical Doctrine* (Grand Rapids, MI: Zondervan, 1994), 21.

your own journey Home. Not surprisingly, there is an applicable passage for each aspect of the heart formation as you grow. It is my prayer that these short snippets from *The Pilgrim's Progress* will spark your interest and spur you on to read it in its entirety. In the following passage Christian's traveling companion, Faithful, is defending himself and the Christianity he holds.

FAITHFUL. May I speak a few words in my own defence?

JUDGE. Sirrah, sirrah, thou deservest to live no longer, but to be slain immediately upon the place; yet, that all men may see our gentleness towards thee, let us hear what thou, vile runagate, hast to say.

FAITHFUL. 1. I say, then, in answer to what Mr. Envy hath spoken, I never said aught but this, that what rule, or laws, or custom, or people, were flat against the word of God, are diametrically opposite to Christianity. If I have said amiss in this, convince me of my error, and I am ready here before you to make my recantation. 2. As to the second, to wit, Mr. Superstition, and his charge against me, I said only this, that in the worship of God there is required a divine faith; but there can be no divine faith without a divine revelation of the will of God. Therefore, whatever is thrust into the worship of God that is not agreeable to divine revelation, cannot be done but by a human faith; which faith will not be profitable to eternal life. 3. As to what Mr. Pickthank hath said, I say, (avoiding terms, as that I am said to rail, and the like,) that the prince of this town, with all the rabblement, his attendants, by this gentleman named, are more fit for a being in hell than in this town and country. And so the Lord have mercy upon me.[4]

### *Personal Spiritual Discipleship: Worship*

Worship is the heartfelt expression of love, adoration, honor, veneration, and reverence toward God. Wayne Grudem defined worship as "the activity of glorifying God in His presence with our voices and hearts."[5] It is giving God all we are—hearts, heads, and hands—every day until He returns or calls us home (Rom. 12:1). Even mute creation declares God's glory: everything He has made proclaims it. The unavoidable contrast of the omnipotent, infinite God with our own weak and temporal selves should lead us to fall before Him in worship. Indeed, a cursory glance at the cultures of the world reveals that while they have a religion of some kind and worship something, their expression will

---

[4] John Bunyan, *The Pilgrim's Progress* (1678), see https://dailylit.com/read/14-the-pilgrims-progress?page=31.

[5] Grudem, *Systematic Theology*, 1,003.

never be biblical worship of the true God without hearing gospel proclamation and teaching. We live in a worshipping world that is lost and hell-bound unless it hears the good news of the gospel. God's self-revelation is what they need to hear.

The Bible is our textbook for worship. From as early as the time that Adam and Eve had Seth, who fathered Enosh, men began to call on Yahweh. Noah built an altar and worshipped God with a burnt offering after the floodwaters receded. Abram built an altar to the Lord in Bethel and called on the name of the Lord. He declared to the servants when he intended to offer Isaac as a sacrifice, "Stay here with the donkey. The boy and I will go over there *to worship*; then we'll come back to you" (Gen. 22:5, emphasis added). Moses worshipped God and received God's specific requirements for Israel to guide them in their worship of Him. In the Ten Commandments, God forbade us to worship other gods (Exod. 20:3–6). He established the tabernacle, and eventually the temple in Jerusalem, as the place of worship and sacrifice, giving His people guidelines for how to worship Him rightly. God warned them of the great sin of worshipping other gods, promised judgment if they did, and followed through on that promise by punishing them when they rebelled against Him. God also blessed those who refused to worship other gods. The story of Shadrach, Meshach, and Abednego is a powerful narrative demonstration of the honor that God gives to those who remain faithful worshippers of a faithful God.

The book of Psalms was the hymnal and worship guide for Israel and has served as such for the church. David and the other psalmists sing hymns of praise, thanksgiving, and prayers of petition. The psalms serve as a guide for all who want to know the heart of worship, whether in corporate expression of the temple or the personal worship from a shepherd boy giving thanks to the Almighty for deliverance from danger.

In the New Testament we see that the devil tempted Jesus to sin by promising Him the world if He would just worship him. Jesus reminded him, and every reader of the Gospels since, that God's people are to worship God and God alone. Jesus also taught at length to correct the Pharisees' false worship. They had replaced God as the object and recipient of their worship by giving honor to one another. They prayed to themselves and kept rules of their own making to achieve self-righteousness, and they created a religion that worshipped and honored its creators. Perhaps many of the Pharisees were good men blinded by the accepted system of the day and were unintentionally deceived into thinking that their efforts were genuine worship of God; after all, that is what the religious rulers required. Sadly, by very definition, anyone who is deceived doesn't know that they are. Paul declared that worship was not just the offering of a portion of our goods; it is heartfelt devotion of our entire lives to God. "Therefore, brothers, by the mercies of God, I urge you to present your bodies as a living sacrifice, holy and pleasing to God; this is your spiritual worship" (Rom. 12:1).

To guard against demonic deception as seen in false religions and cults, we must worship according to what God has revealed in the Bible. Constant vigilance is required, evaluating our worship by what we find in the Word, being careful not to simply worship Him as we imagine or as false, traditional religions guided us in the past. To truly worship God we must know Him, and to truly know Him we must know His Word, being guided by the Holy Spirit to understand it. That means that to know and worship Him truly, we must be born again and be filled with His Spirit.

Jesus taught the Samaritan woman at the well whom we should worship and how.

> Jesus told her, "Believe Me, woman, an hour is coming when you will worship the Father neither on this mountain nor in Jerusalem. You Samaritans worship what you do not know. We worship what we do know, because salvation is from the Jews. But an hour is coming, and is now here, when the true worshipers will worship the Father in spirit and truth. Yes, the Father wants such people to worship Him. God is spirit, and those who worship Him must worship in spirit and truth." (John 4:21–24)

In the New Testament we learn that Jesus is the true Temple, the true Sacrifice, and the Object of true worship. True worship of the Father must be done according to His Word, in the Spirit, and in Truth. All who claim to be worshipping God the Father, but who do not worship the Son and the Spirit as God, are not worshipping the God of the Bible. The true and living God has revealed Himself as the Triune God.

The book of Revelation also gives great insight into true worship. Such worship should flow freely from the hearts and minds of God's people. True worship there is contrasted with the false worship of false deities and demons, which will always exist in the absence of true worship of the one true God.

Worship that flows from a heart after God's own heart, with the mind of Christ, and the indwelling presence of the Holy Spirit does not have to be forced or faked; indeed it cannot. Rather, it is the natural outflow of living in love with God. Don Whitney wrote, "Worship often includes words and actions, but it goes beyond them to the focus of the mind and heart."[6] As we practice God's presence, worship is the expression of emotions that flood our hearts and minds, not just the logical consequence of what such a Savior deserves, although both are involved in balanced biblical worship.

---

[6] Donald Whitney, *Spiritual Disciplines for the Christian Life* (Colorado Springs, CO: NavPress, 2014), 106.

Public worship is essential in the life of a Christian (Heb. 10:25), but it can never be the only time that we worship God. If the only time that the pastor worships God is in church on Sunday, the public worship that he leads will be weak. Certainly public worship is modeled and commanded in the Bible, but it was never to be the only time we worship. Daily worship at a personal level should be evident in a Christian's life.

Walking in communion with God daily, living in love with Jesus, and abiding in His Word result in a lifestyle of prayer. Such a person worships God continually, not just on Sunday mornings in public or corporate worship. While a godly man leads his family in daily prayer and family worship, he also practices private worship. During his devotional time with the Lord each day reading his Bible and praying, the pastor should focus his heart and mind on God and enter into a time of private worship.

Spending time with those we love is an expression of our love. We share with them our deepest fears, greatest joys, and even the mundane details of everyday life. In this way we come to know them, and they come to know us; in fact, the more time we spend with them, we even tend to take on personality traits, share values, and embrace similar ideas about life. Such blessings attend the spending of focused time in worship of God as well. Wayne Grudem listed some results and blessings of genuine worship: we delight in God, we draw near to God, He draws near to us, we sense His ministry to us, and we see His enemies flee.[7] As we share life together with loved ones, we grow in depth of fellowship through communion, causing our love and appreciation for them to grow. This same principle is true in our time with God, but it is much richer. With God, we add the growing dimension of recognizing His worth and telling Him of our love and thankfulness, confessing our need for Him, and meditating on His attributes.

Declaring to Him the worth at which we value Him is a vital component of worship. We will always be growing in our appreciation of Him and His worth because He is infinite, eternal, and well . . . God. Worship is ascribing worth to Him, hence the Old English word *woerthship,* or "worth-ship." In other words, one way to measure the depth of worship you give to God daily is to consider the question, *What is God worth to me?* Imagine a pair of old-fashioned balancing scales, the kind used by merchants to measure out everything from grain to gold. If God were placed on one side of the scale of your values, importance, and worth, what would you have to place on the other side to balance Him out? All of the universe placed on the other side should not be able to lift God from the weight of glory that you see in Him. God's proper value or worth is infinite.

When challenged by friends and family not to give up his future, fame, and wealth to go to the mission field,

---

[7] Grudem, *Systematic Theology,* 1,005–9.

reasoning that God would surely not expect so much, C. T. Studd responded, "If Jesus be God and He died for my sin, no sacrifice I could make would be too great." What is God worth to you? As you express to Him the value that He has in your life, you are worshipping Him.

Certainly God has a place of great worth in your life and in the lives of those you teach and disciple. As true believers we love Him and want to grow in our relationship with Him. So why spend time teaching Christians that this should be a fundamental component of their lives? Unfortunately, we cannot assume any level of spiritual formation; rather, we must model, mentor, and mold others to value daily worship of the Lord. The "shoulds and oughts" are not automatic in a fallen world. Personal worship is a discipline, and just like any healthy discipline, we must train ourselves until it becomes habit and then continue to discipline ourselves as an ingrained pattern of life. We must strive to keep the world from forcing us into its mold and instead earnestly seek to become like Jesus, becoming conformed to His image. Don Whitney wrote that worship is a spiritual discipline that is both "an end and a means. The worship of God is an *end* in itself because to worship, as we've defined it, is to focus on and respond to God. . . . But worship is also a *means* in the sense that it is a means to godliness."[8] We must strive after worship. God deserves it; He demands it; He forbids granting it

---

[8] Whitney, *Spiritual Disciplines for the Christian Life*, 114.

to another. Moreover, He knows that our sincere, single-minded focus on Him enables us to worship in a way that becomes a pathway to peace and joy for us.

Pastoral training must include guidance in *whom* to worship. This is important because, as we have noted, everyone already worships something. The initial embracing of Christianity should not be merely placing a cross on top of whatever was believed prior to the preaching of the gospel. It is helpful to understand the *why* and the *when* of worship, why we should worship Him and *when*, regarding the importance of practicing this discipline daily. The *where* of personal worship shows us that this does not only happen in church or our place of daily devotions, but can be practiced wherever we are throughout the day. The *how* of personal worship teaches us the ways that personal worship differs from corporate worship. As you are being trained and taught through this portion of *Hearts, Heads, & Hands*, spend some time praising God for His attributes in personal worship and thanking Him for what He has done for you personally and throughout history.

Worship flows from our entire being and not just from our minds. All of our senses are often engaged in worshipful settings. For instance, sitting in the ordered beauty of a high-ceilinged sanctuary with dark wood pews and stained-glass windows; hearing the sounds of well-tuned instruments accompanying beautiful harmonies of praise music; smelling the fragrance of aged wood, flowers, and candles, and holding your well-worn Bible can help to promote a worshipful attitude. Even when you are alone at home, the senses can still be employed to enhance worship.

One's environment can impact times of worship in many ways. A sense of order in the place of worship is much more conducive than cluttered chaos. Walking outside through a field or along a forest trail, or even down the streets of the neighborhood, are ways to commune with God during prayer and worship. We should structure our place of prayer to avoid distractions and interruptions as much as possible, yet we should never become so dependent on such arrangements that we cannot worship God when distractions are present. Many have found that music is a powerful way to enhance times of personal worship. Music certainly had an enormous influence and place in David's life. Many of the greatest theologians throughout Christian history also were composers of hymns. Today, many keep a hymnal near their place for daily quiet time and worship by singing a hymn or two as they spend time with God. Even if your devotional spot does not allow for singing, you can read through a hymn and sing it softly or in your mind. If you do not have access to a hymnal, you may have a variety of worship songs memorized. This is a practice you can easily exercise. The most important thing is to make personal worship of God a daily discipline.

## *The Fruit of the Spirit: Peace*

> ". . . the Pilgrim they laid in a large upper
> chamber, whose window opened toward the sun-
> rising; the name of the chamber was Peace; where
> he slept till break of day. . . ."[9]

Paul wrote to the Galatians that the fruit in the life of a man filled with the Spirit is love, joy, peace, patience, kindness, goodness, faith, gentleness, and self-control. Of these, we have considered the aspects of love and joy already; now we turn towards peace. This peace described stems from knowing and doing God's will, growing in grace, developing a fuller understanding of His Word, and living in fellowship with Him. Isaiah said, "You will keep the mind that is dependent on You in perfect peace, for it is trusting in You" (Isa. 26:3).

All of the personal spiritual disciplines flow together in perfect harmony as they were provided to us from God. As we develop the fruit of the Spirit in our lives, we must remember that it is not an achievement that we reach by our efforts alone; rather, God works through us to bring us to the place where He longs for us to be. The pastor's thought life that we consider in each week's heart knowledge is couched in the peace of God. Paul demonstrated the thought life and peace in this way:

---

[9] Bunyan, *The Pilgrim's Progress,* https://dailylit.com/read/14-the-pilgrims-progress?page=16.

Don't worry about anything, but in everything,
through prayer and petition with thanksgiving,
let your requests be made known to God. And the
peace of God, which surpasses every thought, will
guard your hearts and minds in Christ Jesus.

Finally brothers, whatever is true, whatever
is honorable, whatever is just, whatever is pure,
whatever is lovely, whatever is commendable—if
there is any moral excellence and if there is any
praise—dwell on these things. Do what you have
learned and received and heard and seen in me,
and the God of peace will be with you. (Phil.
4:6–9)

Paul teaches that the peace of God will guard our
hearts and minds because the God of peace will be with us.

A mind saturated with the Bible is able to call God's
promises quickly to mind in any crisis. Someone walking
in step with the Spirit does not tiptoe through life on egg-
shells, breathing shallow breaths in anxious fear, but rather
boldly strides into God's plan in each moment that comes,
knowing that He has a plan and is in sovereign control.
Such knowledge gives peace to embrace His plan and go
forth boldly! Jim Elliot wrote, "Wherever you are, be all
there! Live to the hilt every situation you believe to be the
will of God." Only someone living in the peace that the
knowledge of God's sovereignty brings may have the confidence to live this way.

Peace of mind is so elusive that those who lack it may question the sanity of those who exhibit it. Yet peace is not the absence of crisis; it is the presence of Christ. It is hard to preach about God's sovereignty and casting every care on the One who cares for us while we are living in anxiety and suffering panic attacks. A life at peace in the midst of chaos is evidence of the Spirit within. A Spirit-filled Christian should be the opposite of those little snow globes that we shake to create a lovely winter scene with snow falling on a country church on Christmas Eve. The room in which you sit may be softly lit by candles and warmed by a glowing fireplace with Christmas carols in the background, but inside that little snow globe there is a blizzard coming down! Christians are to be the opposite of that. With us, even though all around us is disaster, danger, and chaos, we are to be at peace, trusting in the unseen hand of our sovereign God. The pastor should model such calm and peace in his daily life so much that it attracts others to want to know how he has such peace. That is only possible when the Spirit fills the heart and produces the fruit of peace. We cannot blame circumstances of life for our character and attitude. Trials and difficulties give us opportunities to demonstrate the peace that only the Spirit can bring. Vance Havner said, "What is down in the well will come up in the bucket!"[10] The hardships do not make us who we are; they reveal who we are.

## *The Pastor's Thought Life: Just*

Paul instructed believers to discipline their thought lives to correct the negative, stinking-thinking cycles that hamper our efforts to honor Christ. We have already considered what Paul wrote to the Philippians about thinking on whatever things are true and honorable. This week we consider his exhortation to think on whatever things are just. When we think about what is just, or right, or fair, we stop focusing on ourselves. A principle cause for our anxious, disordered lives is our efforts to manipulate and maneuver for selfish ambition. A good practice to develop is frequent consideration of a simple question: What is the right thing to do? This should guide our thinking, because the Judge of all the earth will always do what is just and right (Gen. 18:25), and seeking to be like Him is our goal.

When Paul wrote to encourage the Philippians, he told them that he was eager to send Timothy to them.

> Now I hope in the Lord Jesus to send Timothy to you soon so that I also may be encouraged when I hear news about you. For I have no one else like-minded who will genuinely care about your interests; all seek their own interests, not those of

[10] Vance Havner, *Pepper 'n Salt* (Grand Rapids, MI: Fleming R. Revell, 1966).

Jesus Christ. But you know his proven character,
because he has served with me in the gospel
ministry like a son with a father. (Phil. 2:19–22)

Timothy had proven himself to be one who was not
selfishly looking out for his own personal gain and inter-
ests. In the same way, the pastor should be concerned
about justice for his flock. Matters of social justice, religious freedom, discrimination, legal rights, and whatever
is just should burden him. He stands for the oppressed
(Prov. 19:17; 21:13; 24:11). Remember that Jesus zeal-
ously defended equal access to God when He cleansed the
temple (Mark 11:17). He declared that His Father's house
was to be a house of prayer for all nations, yet they had
turned the court of the Gentiles into a marketplace that
effectively excluded non-Jews from access to God in that
day. Our churches continue this kind of abuse when they
allow prejudice or discrimination to discourage or deny
people of other races, socioeconomic statuses, or literacy
levels access to  God in our evangelism, discipleship, and
worship.

The reshaping of the thought life is in this section of
personal spiritual disciplines because it is not easy or automatic. We must struggle to deny the selfish tendencies that
are instilled in us and have been nurtured from an early
age. The most natural thing for fallen humanity to do is to
look out for self and ask, "What's in it for me?" This leads
to much anxious thought.

The shepherd of God's flock is concerned for what is just. Growing in Christlikeness encourages this concern since He both modeled and taught it. Yet, this thinking about "what is just" may easily bring about distress when we remember that we will stand before the righteous Judge one day. Most of us would not want to be treated justly, that is, to get what we deserve. If we received what we deserved, none of us could stand. But including in our thinking that which is *true, honorable, and just* gives us hope: the Son of God died in our place so that our just God could justify ungodly rebels, as we were. He was completely honorable in doing so since Jesus honored the law in every respect and never sinned. As the fully righteous One, true and just, He willingly went to the cross to pay for our sin and to give us His righteousness, without which no one will see the Lord. To think on the just One who fulfilled all righteousness so that we may be considered just ones as well brings deep and abiding peace. Let that which is just be a familiar theme in your thought life.

## The Head: Christian Doctrine

And He personally gave some to be apostles,
some prophets, some evangelists, some pastors
and teachers, for the training of the saints in the
work of ministry, to build up the body of Christ,
until we all reach unity in the faith and in the
knowledge of God's Son, growing into a mature

man with a stature measured by Christ's fullness. Then we will no longer be little children, tossed by the waves and blown around by every wind of teaching, by human cunning with cleverness in the techniques of deceit. (Eph. 4:11–14)

During my time as a missionary in Ecuador, I would often teach an all-day workshop in local churches entitled "Basic Bible Doctrines." The people were very interested and seemed to profit by it, but I always felt it was too inadequate for all they really needed to know. In fact it was, but it was at least a good primer and an introduction that often whetted their appetites for more education. The material specifically dedicated to theology outlined in this module is not much more than that. But we have been gratified to see that graduates from our basic cycle desire to continue their education and request advanced training.

To students who feel that this is just too basic a course and desire more information, let me say that I fully agree. As you grow in your desire to learn more, speak with your instructor and ask him for recommendations on how you can continue to increase your theological training after this week's course. A course such as this week's instruction will hopefully spur you on to desire more, provide a basic foundation on which to build future teaching, and harmonize with the theology you learned in the Old and New Testament overviews. These are simply foundational doctrines that we want you to know and be able to explain.

## Biblical or Systematic

What we are to believe about God can be presented in two different ways. One approach is biblical theology, and the other is systematic theology. Biblical theology presents doctrines and concepts as they are revealed progressively through the Scriptures, beginning in the Pentateuch and continuing to the end of the Bible. Systematic theology gathers all that God has revealed in His Word, considers the reflections of men in theological writings, biblical commentaries, and church councils, and presents it to the student under headings or categories.

The advantage of biblical theology is seeing the unfolding of the redemptive narrative as you study the Bible. The unity and harmony of all of the parts of the Bible can be appreciated as progressive revelation is noted, and all that God teaches in the Word can be embraced—and can correct false, traditional religious beliefs—incrementally, chapter by chapter, book by book, and section by section. Since many of you may be studying the Bible in-depth for the first time, the biblical theological approach would be logical.

The advantage of systematic theology for teaching in short-term courses is that the categories allow for easier division and instruction of the doctrines. Many pastors are already familiar with some of the doctrines and ask questions specifically related to them. Systematic theology allows them to consider each doctrine at greater depth in the time allowed. An obvious benefit of gathering Christian doctrines under categorical headings is that this approach presents biblical revelation, conclusions from church councils, and two thousand years of theological reflection, research, and writing.

In the Old and New Testament overviews, we sought to trace five key biblical teachings throughout every book of the Bible. In doing so, it is hoped that you have already noted the unity, harmony, and consistency of the Bible. In this chapter the approach is predominantly under doctrinal headings, but when teaching others you should feel the freedom to walk through the Bible and show section by section how the full doctrine was revealed incrementally, adding to that the reflections of theologians and conclusions of church councils. All teachers should always have the freedom to utilize the method that presents the necessary doctrines best in their context.

## Liberation Theology

Many of the contexts for pastoral training are in areas where there are marginalized, disenfranchised people. In fact, a primary reason why this training model is popular among them is because of its accessibility, affordability, and availability. Many people in the world are unreached because they are in hard-to-reach places, hidden in pockets of poverty or oppression, and speak languages other than that of the dominant cultural class. In such contexts liberation theology finds fertile soil. Marxist and socialistic political teachings filter into the minds and hearts of people, and when they hear the gospel, it is heard through the filter of that worldview and context. Some social activists have injudiciously used the Bible and manipulated teachings of Christianity to foment change.

Liberation theology is commonly found wherever there are oppressed peoples and has resulted in Latin American, black, feminine, Asian, and Native American liberation theology. It is not as much concerned with teaching a set of timeless doctrinal beliefs as it is in devising and proof-texting arguments to facilitate social change. "[Liberation theology] is more a movement that attempts to unite theology and sociology concerns than a new school of theological theory."[11] God is presented as having a preferential option for the poor, and Christ is always on their side, leading them in social and political change. It presents a theological system that reinterprets the teachings of Jesus through the lives and realities of the oppressed. This brief snippet to introduce liberation theology is included only because it often influences the contexts of Christianity where we train pastors. This simple description is not meant to be sufficient for understanding such a complex theological system or to insinuate that it is the only worldview that needs to be considered while teaching. Module 6 will include an overview of the major world religions and some forms of animism that

---

[11] Walter A. Elwell, *Evangelical Dictionary of Theology* (Grand Rapids, MI: Baker, 2001), 635.

will also be encountered. With that brief context we now turn our attention to the core aspects of Christian doctrine.

## *The Doctrine of Revelation*[12]

This section on the doctrine of revelation refers to specific revelation, the Bible itself, and not to the general revelation seen in creation (Ps. 19:1–4; Rom. 1:18–20). This doctrine helps us to have confidence in the Bible's authority, to understand that it is the Word of God and that it contains all we need for faith and practice. The Bible was given through the inspiration of the Holy Spirit to at least forty different human authors, in three languages, over a period covering more than fifteen hundred years. The inspiration of the Bible refers to the truth that it is "God-breathed" (2 Tim. 3:16 NIV). While God sometimes gave words to men directly, indeed even with the command to write down in a book what He was saying (Exod. 17:14), the whole of the Bible is not recorded dictation from God. Nor was it given in a mechanical sense where the author went into a trance and God used him like a ballpoint pen to write His words. Neither was the inspiration like that of a poet who is inspired to write a love sonnet. Rather, the

---

[12] The content and divisions for this chapter are drawn principally from Wayne Grudem, *Christian Beliefs: Twenty Basics Every Christian Should Know* (Grand Rapids, MI: Zondervan, 2005); Grudem, *Systematic Theology*; and Louis Berkhof, *Manual of Christian Doctrine* (Grand Rapids, MI: Eerdmans, 2009).

Holy Spirit utilized the personalities and vocabularies of the authors while superintending the accurate communication of God's thoughts and messages into static form with pen and ink on paper (1 Cor. 2:13; 2 Pet. 1:21).

## CANON

The books of the Bible were formally accepted into the canon of Scripture, which is a collection of sixty-six books—thirty-nine in the Old Testament and twenty-seven in the New Testament. The word *canon* is a Greek word that means "rule or standard," and in this case it refers to the books that are accepted as the authoritative divine books to be included in the Old and New Testament collections. These books were decided on by early church fathers and church councils. They did not bestow the authority on the sixty-six books; they only recognized that these met all the criteria for inclusion. Since the closing of the canon, there is no longer any need for further revelation or fresh words from God in addition to the Bible. The Apocrypha is not part of the canon.

## AUTHORITY

The authority of Scripture refers to the fact that the Bible is the Word of God and to disbelieve any part of the Bible is to disbelieve God Himself. "In the Old Testament, the words 'the Lord said,' 'the Lord spoke,' and 'the word of the Lord came,' are used 3,808 times." The Bible itself claims to be the Word of God, and the Holy Spirit persuades us as He illumines our minds in the reading of it (1 Cor. 2:13–14). Since the Bible is the Word of God, it is without error and does not ever affirm anything that is untrue (Ps. 19:7–11). Jesus taught that the Scripture cannot be broken (John 10:35) and affirmed stories of the Old Testament as facts—such as the reality of Adam and Eve, Noah and the ark during a worldwide flood, and Jonah being swallowed by a large fish.

## CLARITY

We refer to the clarity of Scripture when we declare that although there are parts that are hard to understand (2 Pet. 3:16), the Bible is clear for leading us to salvation. The theological term for this doctrine is *the perspicuity of Scripture*, which simply means that the Bible is clear enough to be understood by anyone who reads it and seeks God's help in the process (Pss. 119:18; 130; 1 Cor. 1:18; 2:14). This doctrine of the clarity of Scripture does not claim that believers will always arrive at the same conclusion and interpretation of the Bible. Because we process truth through divergent worldviews and because of sin, there will always be differences of opinion and even division among Bible scholars.

## NECESSITY

If God had not revealed Himself in His Word, we would know nothing definitive about Him. Through creation, i.e. general revelation, we would know that He exists, that we are sinners, and that there is life after this life (Ps. 19:1–4; Rom. 1:18–20; 2:14, 15; Eccles. 3:11), but we would know nothing else about Him. Therefore it was essential that He reveal Himself in His Word. The Bible is necessary in order for us to understand even general revelation. Jesus said that we live by every word that comes from the mouth of God (Matt. 4:4). We need the Word of God to know Him and to know how to be saved (Rom. 10:13–17; 2 Tim. 3:15). We certainly need the truth, and Jesus said, "Your word is truth" (John 17:17).

## Sufficiency

Christians neither need nor give authority to any books beyond the Bible. Cults and false world religions may embrace the Old and New Testaments as religious books with valuable moral teachings, but they do not recognize their authority or sufficiency. They add to the Bible other teachings that they believe are necessary. The Christian holds that the Bible alone is sufficient for the knowledge we need. Its teachings are sufficient for what we need to be saved and to live in obedience to God (Deut. 29:29). There is nothing required of Christians that is not found in His Word.

## *The Doctrine of the Nature and Attributes of God*

Every culture in the world has some understanding of a creator god. Both the inner sense that God has given to every one of us, and nature itself, declare that He exists

(Rom. 1:19–25). While this knowledge is sufficient to con-
demn mankind, since all seek to suppress the revelation
they have seen and exchange the worship of the Creator
for the worship of created things, the testimony of creation
is not sufficient to save us. We must know and be known
by God. Since it is impossible to know Him truly simply
through nature, we must study what He has revealed about
Himself. While we may know Him truly, His incomprehen-
sibility renders us incapable of knowing Him fully in this
life.

What is He like? What has He commanded us to be
like? These questions lead us to inquire about His characteristics or attributes. Some of these attributes are true of
God alone, and others we are to strive to emulate in our
own lives. We refer to these as *incommunicable* and *communicable* attributes.[13]

*Incommunicable* attributes refer to those that describe
Him alone. His *independence* means He does not need
us or anything else (Acts 17:24–25), yet He allows us to
have fellowship with Him, glorify Him, and love Him (Isa.
43:7). His *immutability* refers to the fact that He never
changes. If He did, He would be going from inferior to
better, or declining in perfection. The psalmist praises God
for the fact that He never changes (Ps. 102:25–27). The

---

[13] The following treatment is only a partial illustrative listing of the communicable and incommunicable attributes of God.
For a more exhaustive treatment as well as a fuller explanation
please refer to Grudem, Berkhof, or Erickson.

God who is perfect and never changes declared, "Because I, Yahweh, have not changed, you descendants of Jacob have not been destroyed" (Mal. 3:6; see also Matt. 5:48). His promises never change, He cannot lie, and His faithfulness endures forever. His *eternity* speaks of the truth that He had no beginning and will never have an end (Ps. 90:2). At any point in eternity past, the present, or eternity future, He eternally is. Closely related to this are the *immensity* and the *infinity* of God; i.e., He has no measure or limit (1 Kings 8:27; Jer. 23:23–24).

God's *omnipotence* speaks of His infinite divine power to carry out His will. While there are some things that God cannot do, such as lie, die, change, sin, and deny Himself, He can do all His holy will. No one can thwart His will or stay His hand because He is all-powerful (Job 9:12; Jer. 32:17; Matt. 19:26; Eph. 1:11; 3:20; Rev. 4:11). God is *omnipresent*, which is to say that He is at once everywhere in every place (Ps. 139:7–10).

He is *invisible* and no one has ever seen Him (John 1:18). He is *omniscient*, all knowing, completely *wise*, knowing *Himself* and all things (Rom. 16:27; Job 12:13). He knows everything there is to know (1 John 3:20). Nothing and no one are hidden from His eyes. Everything is laid bare before Him (Heb. 4:13). God never comes to know anything, but rather intuitively knows everything including any word we will say before it is even on our tongue (Ps. 139:4, 16). We may also speak of the *simplicity* or the *unity* of God. This refers to the fact that God cannot be divided into parts; His divine essence is not a composite whole of other ingredients and distinct attributes added together.

The *holiness* of God refers to His moral perfection and that He is separate from all that is not morally perfect. He is perfect in His holiness (Exod. 15:11; 1 Sam. 2:2; Isa. 57:15; Hos. 11:9). This ethical holiness means that considering His perfection is overwhelming to our sense of sinfulness by comparison (Job 34:10; Isa. 6:5; Hab. 1:13). He is altogether righteous, and His perfection demands that He require justice for every violation of His holiness (Deut. 32:4). He is *Spirit* and does not have a body like men (John 4:24); thus there is no limitation to God regarding size or dimensions.

God's *communicable* attributes refer to those that we may share, or at least those with which we share some analogous attributes, but those true of human beings are limited and imperfect in comparison with God. God is *truthful* and cannot lie (Jer. 10:10). Closely related to this is His *faithfulness* and that He will always honor what He has said (Num. 23:19). He is completely and always steadfast in His *goodness*. This benevolence of God is shown to His creation in acts of loving-kindness (Pss. 36:6; 145:8–9, 16; Matt. 5:45; 6:26; Acts 14:17). Jesus taught the rich young ruler that no one but God is truly good (Luke 18:19). As a perfectly good God, He is also the source of every truly good thing we have (Pss. 73:25; 84:11; Gen. 1:31; James 1:17).

The *love* of God is often highlighted as the primary attribute of God, at least by popular religiosity. Yet this attribute is no more or less true or important than the others. John wrote that God is love (1 John 4:8), and His love may be considered from various perspectives such as the grace, mercy, and longsuffering of God.

The *grace* of God is His unmerited favor toward those who not only can do nothing to earn it, but do not even desire it when He first stirs their hearts (Eph. 1:6–7; 2:7–9; Titus 2:11; 3:4–7).

*Justice* is when we receive from the Lord what we deserve; *mercy* is when we do not receive the punishment that we deserve; and *grace* is when we receive good from Him in place of the punishment that we deserve. *Mercy* from God is not based on what we deserve, but is full of pity; yet, this is only possible from a just God based on the merits of Christ on our behalf (Luke 1:54, 72, 78; Rom. 9:16; 15:9; Eph. 2:4). He is *longsuffering,* which is exhibited by His patient love and his forbearing our continuance in sin even though He has warned us repeatedly and has received countless promises from us that we will not sin in such ways again (Rom. 2:4; 9:22; 1 Pet. 3:20; 2 Pet. 3:15).

## *The Doctrine of the Trinity*

The doctrine of the Trinity is found throughout the Bible even though the word *Trinity* is not (Deut. 6:4–5; Pss. 45:6–7; 110:1; Matt. 3:16–17; 28:19). This doctrine teaches that the one God exists in three persons—Father,

Son, and Holy Spirit—in tri-unity (John 1:1–2; 14:26). These persons are each fully God and, as such, are eternal and share the same attributes and essential nature. Christians do not believe in three Gods, nor in one God who manifests Himself in various forms at different times for different purposes. The Council of Nicea in AD 325 affirmed that Christ is of the same nature as the Father, denouncing Arianism as heresy (Col. 2:9). Arianism is the erroneous teaching that the Son was a created being, reiterated today in the heresy of Jehovah's Witnesses. The Council of Constantinople in AD 381 affirmed the deity of the Holy Spirit. Although the persons are equal, there is a functional subordination, as when Jesus prayed to the Father and deferred to His will.

The doctrine of the Trinity is an essential doctrine. Without the deity of each person of the Trinity, the doctrines of the atonement and justification by faith, just as two examples among many, would be baseless and fatally flawed. Even so, the doctrine of the Trinity is difficult to understand and to explain to others. A word of caution is in order here. Some try to use illustrations to explain the Trinity, but most illustrations are inadequate and can unintentionally teach error. For instance, one common illustration is that of an apple: You have the skin of the apple, the fruit of the apple, and the seeds. Some will say that God can be thus described, but this results in an unlawful separation and division of the members of the Godhead. It would be possible to have skin and seeds without the fruit or the fruit and seeds without the skin. But it is impossible to separate the three persons of the triune Godhead in this way. Others have used the illustration of water saying that you could have ice, liquid, or steam, but they are all forms of water. This is modalism, a teaching that God is one Person who simply manifests Himself in different forms at different times, which is a heresy to be avoided. Likewise, some would use the illustration that I am a son, a husband, and a father, but I am one person. This is also modalism. These truths are too crucial to be risked with inadequate illustrations.

## The Doctrine of Creation

God created the universe and everything in it *ex nihilo*, out of nothing. He spoke it into existence with the power of His word, and it was declared to be very good (Gen. 1; 2; Col. 1:16; Rev. 4:11). God made all that exists, and it is dependent on Him. If He should withhold the might of His power for one instant, all that is would fly apart and cease to be (Job 12:10; Acts 17:28; Col. 1:17). He Himself is distinct from His creation, being transcendent and immanent. Even though this is a fallen world that now produces unnatural disasters such as hurricanes, earthquakes, volcanic eruptions, and tsunamis, all of creation glorifies God.

## The Doctrine of Providence

The providence of God teaches that God is still involved with His creation, continuing its existence and caring for the universe as He deems best. He directs all that happens in the world and works out all things in accordance with the purpose of His will (Heb. 1:3; Eph. 1:11; Dan. 4:35). Even though God established the universe and His sovereign providence is without limitation, men and women are still responsible for their actions and choices. God is in no way the author of sin, nor does He force anyone to sin against His will (James 1:13). God hears the prayers of His people and works through them, even though very often He uses them to change His people rather than their circumstances.

God's providence sometimes works in supernatural ways that we call miracles. His ongoing immanent involvement in His world is seen in the daily waking from sleep, healing from winter colds, cycles of seasonal change, births of children, and miraculous healings from fatal diagnoses.

## *The Doctrine of the Virgin Birth and Jesus' Humanity*

Jesus Christ is the incarnate Word of God, the second person of the triune Godhead, the Son of God, and our Redeemer who took on flesh and became a man (John 1:14). He was born of the virgin Mary, who had been chosen by God, not because she was sinless through immaculate conception but according to His good pleasure to so choose her. Jesus Christ was fully 100 percent God and 100 percent man, in one person, and He will always be so, world without end. The virgin birth of Christ was necessary for Christ to be born without the taint of original sin but still be fully human, thus fulfilling the necessary requirements for Him to provide our atonement (Rom. 5:18–19; Gal. 4:4–5; 1 Tim. 2:5). As fully human, Christ suffered hunger and thirst, and became tired and sleepy like the rest of us, yet He remained without sin (Heb. 4:15–16).

*Jesus* is the Greek form of the Hebrew name *Joshua*, which means "Yahweh saves." *Christ* is the Greek form of the Hebrew word *Messiah* and means "the anointed one." In the fullness of time He came (Gal. 4:4), being born of a virgin (Matt. 1:18), and fulfilled the plan of the ages to reveal the mystery of how a perfectly righteous God could save sinners like us and remain holy (Rom. 3:26).

## *The Doctrine of Jesus' Deity*

The recognition of Jesus' deity is clearly communicated in the New Testament. He is called God (John 1:1; 20:28), Lord (John 13:13; 20:28), and He spoke of Himself as divine by the use of titles such as "I Am" (John 8:58). In John's revelation Jesus is presented as having omnipotence, eternity, omniscience, and sovereignty, and deserving of worship, all of which are reserved for deity (Rev. 22:13). His full deity is essential for our salvation because only one who is fully God could pay for the sins of mankind; any mere man's death would only pay for his own sin at best (Isa. 53:6; Rom. 3:23). Additionally, the Bible teaches that God saves, not man, thus requiring the One who provides salvation to be God. He also needed to have been God and no mere man because only God could be the mediator between God and man. No man could have done so (1 Tim. 2:5).

## FALSE VIEWS OF HIS DEITY AND HUMANITY

There have been numerous erroneous views regarding the deity of Christ. Such views continue to appear in cults and false religions. Since there is nothing new under the sun, and the devil repeats his lies to the unwary, an awareness of false views identified in history will aid in identifying them when they reappear. A few erroneous views from church history are Apollinarianism, which held that Christ may have had a human body, "but denied that He had a human mind or spirit"; Nestorianism, in which Christ was believed to be two separate persons, one divine and one human; and Monophysitism, which said Christ only had one nature, an enhanced human nature that was not quite divine.

The Council of Chalcedon refuted these false views in AD 451 and affirmed that Jesus Christ was and is the eternal Son of God who had a truly human nature. Moreover, it affirmed that His human and divine natures remained distinct, retaining their own properties, but are eternally and inseparably united together in one person; one nature did some things that the other nature did not, but that anything done by either nature was done by the one person of Christ.

## *The Doctrine of Atonement*

The atonement is the work of Christ to provide our salvation. Christ lived a perfect life and died a vicarious substitutionary death on the cross to make the great exchange of our sin for His perfection, making atonement possible between sinful man and holy God. Because of His *kesed* loving-kindness, God the Father sent His Son, who willingly came to earth and suffered for us to provide our redemption (John 3:16; Rom. 3:25–26). Our atonement required the sinless obedience of Christ (Rom. 5:19) and His suffering our death to pay our sin's penalty (1 Pet. 2:24). The work of Christ for us was prefigured in the Old Testament by the Day of Atonement in Leviticus 16, when the high priest placed his hands on the scapegoat and confessed the sin of the people so that the sin was symbolically transferred to the innocent victim to bear it away. Hebrews 9:22 teaches us that without the shedding of blood there is no remission of sin. The shed blood of Christ is key to understanding the biblical teachings regarding our atonement (Acts 20:28; Rom. 3:25; 5:9; Eph. 1:7; 2:13; Col. 1:20; Heb. 9:14; 1 Pet. 1:2, 19; 1 John 1:7; Rev. 1:5; 5:9). One drop of Jesus' blood would be sufficient to save anyone, but it had to be the last drop; He had to pay what we deserved. Christ willingly suffered and died in our place to earn our atonement.

## *The Doctrine of Jesus' Resurrection and Ascension*

The Bible teaches us that the physical resurrection of Jesus from the grave ensures our regeneration, our justification, and our resurrection from the dead when Christ returns (1 Pet. 1:3; Rom. 4:25; 2 Cor. 4:14). Paul taught that if Christ was not raised from the dead then Christianity is false and powerless, preaching is in vain, our testimony is untrue, forgiveness of sins has not been achieved, and all believers who have died thinking it was all true are lost forever. In short, Christians are the most miserable and pitiable people on earth (1 Cor. 15:14–19). Clearly, Paul and the early Christian church believed Jesus to be raised from the dead (Rom. 1:3–4). Jesus taught the two on the road to Emmaus that His death and resurrection were a key part of the Old Testament's message (Luke 24:25–27). He had already taught His hearers that His resurrection would give credence to His other teachings (Matt. 12:38–40).

Luke ends his Gospel with the ascension of the risen Christ (Luke 24:37–39, 50–53) and picks up there again to begin his subsequent book, The Acts of the Apostles, with an account of Christ's ascending to the Father (Acts 1:9–11). The ascension of Christ hints at our ascension when He returns (1 Thess. 4:17). Christ has gone to prepare a home for us and will receive us one day, upon our death or at His return (John 14:2–3). Now in heaven Christ is seated at the right hand of the Father and intercedes for His own, ruling and reigning from on high.

## Christ's Threefold Office of Prophet, Priest, King

Jesus Christ fulfills the threefold office of Prophet, Priest, and King in all He is for the people of God. As Prophet He speaks God's Word to the church (Deut. 18:15–18). As Priest He represents the people to God, intercedes for them, and makes the required sacrifice for them. As King He provides order, governs, directs, and rules. Christ perfectly fulfills each of these three roles (Rom. 8:34; 1 Cor. 15:25; Heb. 9:11–28; Rev. 19:16).

## The Doctrine of the Holy Spirit

The Holy Spirit is the third Person of the Trinity and is as fully God and eternal as the Father and the Son. He is not merely a power or force; He is a person, and as such He can be lied to and grieved (1 Sam. 16:14; Acts 5:3; Eph. 4:30). He empowers, indwells, and fills believers (Exod. 31:3; Num. 27:18; Judg. 6:34; 1 Sam. 11:6; Matt. 28:19; Acts 1:8; 2:4; 19:6). The Holy Spirit purifies (1 Cor. 6:11), applies the Word and convicts men of its truth and their sin (John 15:26; 16:8), reveals and teaches truth (John 14:26; 2 Pet. 1:21), illumines believers' minds to understand the true meaning of the Word (1 Cor. 2:9–11, 14; Rom. 8:26–27), guides them (John 16:13; Acts 8:29; 11:12; 13:2; 16:7), and assures them that they are God's (Rom. 8:16; Gal. 4:6).

The indwelling presence of the Holy Spirit in a person's life will result in the kind of life that bears the fruit of the Spirit. In the Heart portion of each module, we drill down into each descriptor that Paul used to describe the kind of fruit that springs from the indwelling Spirit. "But the fruit of the Spirit is love, joy, peace, patience, kindness, goodness, faith, gentleness, self-control" (Gal. 5:22–23). The Spirit also gives gifts to believers for the advance and building up of the body of Christ in the world (1 Cor. 12:11, 28–31; 14:1). Not every Christian will possess the same gifts of the Spirit, but all should manifest the same fruit of the Spirit in ever-increasing measure.

## The Doctrine of Humanity and the Fall

### ORIGIN OF MANKIND

God created man and woman in His own image and then declared creation to be very good (Gen. 1:26, 31). The image of God, that aspect of men and women that is moral, spiritual, mental, relational, and creative, was damaged or distorted in man's subsequent fall into sin, but it was not destroyed (Gen. 9:6). While God is spirit and does not have a body like man, mankind has an essential nature made up of the spiritual and the physical (2 Cor. 7:1). Men and women were charged from the very beginning to multiply, fill the earth, and have dominion over it (Gen. 1:28).

God created man and woman and established the human family as the first institution among them. There are at once equality and distinctions seen in men and women from the account of creation. God established creation order, which never changes (1 Cor. 11:3; 1 Tim. 2:13), and which carries over into the family and church leadership; yet, men and women are equal in personhood, value, and importance. They have God-ordained distinct roles in marriage and in the church (Col. 3:18–19). Christians recognize and affirm the equality of man and woman but not sameness, recognizing and affirming the distinct roles they are to hold in the home and the church.

## THE FALL INTO SIN

God created a world that was perfect and very good in every way. Adam and Eve were placed in the Garden of Eden and provided with all that they needed, yet they were tempted by the devil that appeared to them in the form of a serpent. They heeded the temptations of the serpent and fell into sin, which plunged the world and all of their descendants into sin and ruin. The image of God in man that made it so natural to reflect His holiness was now damaged, tarnished, and distorted so that to do so is unnatural among fallen men.

All men and women are born with a sinful nature and are guilty because of Adam's sin. Paul teaches in Romans that Adam's sin was imputed to every person (Rom. 5:12–21). Our sinful nature renders us incapable of avoiding sin, and our nature is fallen from our conception (Ps. 51:1–5). We are not sinners because we have sinned; we sin because we are sinners. We are all guilty by birth and by choice. We have a rebel nature and a rebel record.

Sin brings both guilt and pollution. Not only is there a legal declaration of sin and guilt, but the pollution that comes from sin renders a man corrupt and decreasingly sensitive to God. In the same way that dark sunglasses shield our eyes from the sun's brightness, and increasing the layers of lenses between our eye and the sun blocks out its light more completely, so increasing sins deaden the heart to sensitivity to God (1 Tim. 4:2). Even one sin separates a person from God, who is the holy, righteous Judge (Rom. 3:23), and all the good works we could do would not atone for past sins nor earn forgiveness for future ones (Gal. 3:10).

The fall also plunged the natural world into disaster, resulting in a fallen world where nature is red in tooth and claw, diseases ravage, winds become hurricanes, volcanoes erupt, and earthquakes devastate cities and create tsunamis. None of these things existed before the first Adam and Eve rebelled against God's clear command. The second Adam, Jesus Christ, will bring about a restoration from the effects of the fall.

## The Doctrine of Salvation

"Jesus sought me when a stranger wandering from the fold of God" is not just a line from a hymn we sing in church; it is my testimony and yours. Salvation is from God—His idea and His doing. All we bring to the table is our sin; He provides everything else. Before salvation human beings are dead spiritually, incapable of earning or contributing to their salvation. But God in His mercy brought about our salvation purely by His grace (Eph. 2:1–5). The salvation of men and women is supernatural in every way. God does not cooperate with us to effect our salvation, He alone is the Author and Actor in every step of it. We are not sick and calling for a physician, nor are we drowning and calling for a lifeline. We are dead, life-less at the bottom of the sea, and God reaches down and plucks us out, by His own choice and grace, and breathes life into us.

## The Doctrine of Election

This doctrine is found throughout God's Word to speak of Him choosing some. In the Old Testament we see that He chose Noah, Abram, Isaac, and Jacob over others. He chose the Jews from all the peoples on earth to be His special possession. In the New Testament the word *election* is used to speak of those whom God chooses for salvation (Acts 13:48; Eph. 1:4–6, 12). The Bible teaches that God made this choice before the creation of the universe (Eph. 1:4; Rev. 17:8). Jesus taught, "For many are invited, but few are chosen" (Matt. 22:14; John 6:44, 65).

The knowledge that God has His elect in the world should not discourage evangelism. We should not reason, "The choice has been made, so why bother?" Rather, it should encourage evangelism since we know that God knows His own and He will save them through the preached Word (Rom. 11:5; 2 Thess. 2:13; 2 Tim. 2:10). In fact, even the elect do not come into the world saved; they are elect *unto* salvation, but they must hear the gospel and be born again. The doctrine of election is closely related to the doctrine of *predestination*, which refers to God's sovereign choice, rule, and determination of the lives of men and women (Ps. 139:16; Rom. 9). Remember that Jesus did not come into the world to make salvation *possible*; He came to save sinners by His finished work. "Knowledge of one's election thus brings comfort and joy."[14] We can find peace in knowing that salvation is not by chance or our intelligence and also in knowing that it is not up to our abilities to persuade that make the difference in another's salvation.

## The Doctrine of Effective Calling

God calls and draws men and women to Himself to save them (John 6:44, 65; Rom. 8:30). God calls and draws them to Himself through the use of means, whether that is the preached Word, reading the Bible, gospel presentations in tracts, or an individual's witness. God, who has sovereignly orchestrated all of the events of our lives (Ps. 139:16; Eph. 1:11), uses these events to make external means effectual. God hardens (as with Pharaoh, Exod. 14:4) and softens (as with Lydia, Acts 16:14) the hearts of humans and controls the thoughts and desires of kings (Prov. 16:9; 19:21; 21:1).

---

[14] J. I. Packer, "Election: God Chooses His Own," accessed February 29, 2016, http://www.Monergism.com/thethreshold/articles/onsite/packer/election.html.

Even though we stress God's sovereignty and that He is the one who chooses and calls, no one should nervously fear that although they desire salvation and the forgiveness of their sins, God did not choose and call them so they cannot be saved. Jesus declared, "Come to Me, all of you who are weary and burdened, and I will give you rest. All of you, take up My yoke and learn from Me, because I am gentle and humble in heart, and you will find rest for yourselves. For My yoke is easy and My burden is light" (Matt. 11:28–30). He taught that God loved the world to the degree that He sent His only Son to die for sins and give eternal life and that no one who comes to Him would ever be turned away (John 3:16; 6:37).

## *The Doctrine of Regeneration*

Jesus taught Nicodemus, "I assure you: Unless someone is born again, he cannot see the kingdom of God" (John 3:3). No one can be in a right relationship with God in this life or enter into His presence in the next unless he is regenerated, i.e., born again. The Bible speaks of this change in various ways. Ezekiel spoke of it as God's removing the sinner's heart of stone and replacing it with a heart of flesh (Ezek. 36:26). In the next chapter he recorded a vision about God's putting flesh and sinews on dried-out bones on a valley floor and making them come to life. This is a graphic physical image of what God does spiritually for lost men and women when they are born again. Paul speaks of the regeneration of people as a complete metamorphosis, as when a butterfly comes out of a cocoon completely changed into a new creature—the old has gone and the new has come (2 Cor. 5:17).

## The Doctrine of Conversion

Conversion refers to the ways that people change as a result of a new heart. Although regeneration and conversion are always found together, they must not be confused. God changes our hearts, opens our eyes, unstops our ears, and turns on the light in our darkened minds when He regenerates us, and as a result we flee to Him in conversion. We do not convert to Christ and thus bring about His regeneration of us, i.e., we do not choose Him and place faith in Him to make Him save us. Neither does God regenerate us without our subsequent conversion.

Two aspects of conversion are repentance and faith, and both of these are gifts from God. This involves our willing response to what we have heard preached, the gospel call, placing our faith in Christ, and repenting of our sin and rebellion (John 3:16). All of this would not be possible while spiritually dead, since dead people cannot do anything. True repentance and faith would not be possible without God's first regenerating us, and once He does, we continue repenting and placing faith in Christ for the rest of our lives (Matt. 6:12; Rom. 7:14–24; Gal. 2:20).

### The Doctrine of Saving Faith

This refers to trust and belief in the gospel, not belief simply in the reality of a historical person named Jesus, nor acceptance of a set of facts. The Bible is clear that even demons believe and tremble, but saving faith is not this kind of mere belief in historical facts (James 2:19). Saving faith is believing the message of the gospel and trusting in Jesus Christ (John 1:12; 3:16). Faith is a gift from God (Eph. 2:8) and comes through the Word preached (Rom. 10:17). Faith is a muscle that should be exercised and developed throughout the Christian's life. Saving faith is the key to the mystery of the ages (Heb. 11:1). While so many adherents of the world's religions have tried to earn, sacrifice, and give to achieve spiritual life and salvation, the Bible makes it plain in Habakkuk 2:4, Romans 1:17, and Galatians 3:11 that the righteous live by faith. This became the rallying cry of the Reformation in the 1500s and represented a fresh wind blowing through the dead works of Catholicism. While we do not earn our salvation by works, we must remember that works do have a place in true saving faith (James 2:14, 17). Martin Luther wrote, "We are saved by faith alone, but the faith that saves is never alone." What then should accompany our faith?

### The Doctrine of Repentance

Jesus began His ministry preaching a message of repentance, "Jesus went to Galilee, preaching the good news, of

God: 'The time is fulfilled, and the kingdom of God has come near. Repent and believe in the good news!'" (Mark 1:14–15). Repentance is not simply being sorry for having sinned; it is turning around and walking away from rebellion and into obedience. The Bible speaks of a change of mind that results in new desires and preferences as well as a new hatred for sin and wickedness (2 Cor. 7:9–10). The picture is of a man walking down the road in one direction whose mind is suddenly changed, causing him to turn around and walk in the opposite direction, giving his back to the old desires. When a man truly repents of his sin, he runs to God and pleads for forgiveness and salvation. Repentance involves turning from rebellion against God as well as from anything you trusted in for salvation prior to Christ, and turning to God in obedience and faith (Heb. 6:1).

## *The Doctrine of Justification*

This doctrine speaks of a legal standing before God, which He brought about and in which He sees us as forgiven and declared fully righteous in His sight (Gal. 2:16). He is able to so declare sinners righteous because Jesus earned their righteousness and paid the penalty that every sin deserves. When this atonement is applied to their account, they stand in the position of absolute righteousness, completely justified. Justification means that even though I am actually a sinner, because of all that Jesus has done on my behalf, I may be considered by God as though

I never sinned. This legal declaration by God is not one of fiction; it is a guaranteed status that was earned by Christ (Rom. 3:24; 2 Cor. 5:21). Every sin ever committed must be paid for, but the good news of the gospel is that Jesus paid for every sin I have—or ever will—commit, and the Holy Spirit has applied His payment to my account as I trust in Him and believe the gospel (Rom. 5:1). Now I am no longer under the condemnation of the law, and there is no condemnation stored up for me (Rom. 5:10; 8:1; Eph. 2:16; Col 1:22).

## The Doctrine of Adoption

The good news of the gospel that we may be forgiven of our sins and born again unto eternal life includes the truth also that we are no longer sons of disobedience and children of wrath, but that the Father adopts us into a new family, with Jesus Christ as our elder Brother (Rom. 8:15–17, 23; Eph. 2:2–3; Heb. 2:12, 17). Now we are God's children in His family (1 John 3:2). We have this relationship now, which can never be lost, but we still groan waiting for the fullness of our adoption on the last day (Rom. 8:23–25).

## The Doctrine of Sanctification

Regeneration is a *monergistic*[15] work of God that He performs in us; sanctification is a *synergistic* work that

---

[15] A word meaning that only one is working; not synergistic, where more than one works.

the Holy Spirit works through us and in which we participate (2 Cor. 7:1; Col. 3:1–14; 1 Thess. 4:7; 5:23; Heb. 12:14; 1 Pet. 1:22). In justification we are considered to be instantaneously righteous and perfectly holy legally, but in sanctification we are growing more so. Sanctification is a progressive work by which we grow in holiness and are purified in our hearts and minds in a process that will continue the rest of our lives. Even though believers are now freed from the power of sin (Rom. 6:11–14), we are not free from the presence of sin and will not attain to perfect sinless sanctification in this life (1 Kings 8:46; 1 John 1:8). The Bible teaches that only in heaven will we be free from the presence and hindrance of sin, revealing that we will be perfectly sanctified upon leaving this world (Phil. 3:21; Heb. 12:23; Rev. 14:5; 21:27).

## The Doctrine of Baptism and Filling of the Holy Spirit

The baptism of the Holy Spirit and the filling of the Holy Spirit are not synonymous terms. The baptism of the Holy Spirit is an event that occurs at the moment of salvation and is the work of the Spirit applying to individuals the work of Christ. Believers are immediately indwelled by the Spirit and freed from the power of sin (1 Cor. 12:13). This is a singular occurrence that accompanies justification at salvation. The filling of the Holy Spirit, in contrast, is a work that may be repeated multiple times in a believer's life, referring to times of refreshing, renewed repentance, and rededicated commitment which results in increased sanctification and greater effectiveness in ministry and Christian living.

Christians use these terms variously today, but the points to stress are:

1.  There is no subsequent work of the Holy Spirit whereby one is more or less saved later than they were at conversion.

2.  God's monergistic act of salvation of a sinner is not something that can be or must be repeated. You cannot lose your salvation. The Spirit may be quenched, vexed, and grieved away by sin in the believer's life, and upon repentance the fellowship of the Spirit in fullness may bring sweet times of communion that were impossible while remaining in unrepentant sin, but this is not an indication of re-salvation (Eph. 4:30; 1 Thess. 5:19).

## *The Doctrine of Perseverance of the Saints*

This doctrine teaches that anyone who is truly saved can never lose salvation. God, who began the good work, will carry it on to completion on the Day of Christ Jesus (Phil. 1:6). Of course, if continuation in a right relationship with God were dependent on our efforts, we would fall away totally and finally, but God's power keeps us until the end of life (John 10:27–29; Col. 1:22–23; Jude 24–25). Moreover, many have argued that the eternal life Jesus promised in John 3:16 would not be eternal if it could be lost. Jesus has promised that on the last day He will raise up all who come to Him (John 6:40).

## The Doctrine of Death

Death is the last enemy and a result of the fall (1 Cor. 15:26). For Christians, death is not a punishment, but merely a passageway through which all must pass to be with Christ, which is better than this life could ever offer (1 Cor. 15:54–55; 2 Cor. 5:8; Phil. 1:21–23). Death is not the end of life; at the moment of death, the Christian is made perfect in holiness and is more alive than ever. Certainly, it is the last great change, and so it is sometimes feared simply because the details surrounding it are unknown. Yet, it is simply the laying aside of the body as a cloak no longer needed.

The certainty of death and the sickness and infirmities of old age that often precede it are said to be ways that God loosens our roots from the soil of this world. At the very least, the certainty of death is used by God to cause many to consider their sins seriously and repent. Thomas Watson said, "He may look on death with joy, who can look on forgiveness with faith."[16] John Owen wrote on the *Death of Death in the Death of Christ*, addressing the extent of the atonement and therefore the hope that

---

[16] I. D. E. Thomas, *A Puritan Golden Treasury* (Carlisle, PA: Banner of Truth Trust, 1977), 71.

we have. Hebrews 2:14–15 reminds us that we should have no fear of death: "Now since the children have flesh and blood in common, Jesus also shared in these, so that through His death He might destroy the one holding the power of death—that is, the Devil—and free those who were held in slavery all their lives by the fear of death."

### The Doctrine of the Intermediate State

When a person dies, only their body dies. Normally, we place the bodies of the deceased in a grave, but the soul of the person lives on. But there is a difference between what happens to believers and unbelievers at death. Anyone who has not been born again will immediately enter into a Christless eternity, which tragically is an eternal dwelling place of abject torment. Their bodies remain in the grave until the return of Christ, when their bodies are raised and reunited with their souls for the judgment (Matt. 25:31–46; John 5:28–29; Acts 24:15; Rev. 2:11; 20:12). There will not be any postmortem evangelistic encounter or subsequent opportunity to accept Christ and escape hell. Everyone alive is one breath away from a fixed state of eternity (Heb. 9:27).

When Christians die, their bodies are likewise placed in a grave to await the resurrection, but their souls enter into paradise and the conscious enjoyment of Christ's presence. The Bible speaks of the gospel message as that which frees us from the fear of death and makes the day of leaving this body to be with Christ a thing to be desired (Heb. 2:15;

2 Cor. 5:8; Phil. 1:23). Nonetheless, we may still grieve the loss of friends and family. Tears and sadness are not sinful demonstrations since it is natural to mourn, sometimes for the tragic way in which they died or the loss of their companionship (John 11:35). However, because of the promises of Christ and His Word, though we grieve, we do not grieve as the unbelieving world does (John 14:1–6; 1 Thess. 4:13).

There is no purgatory. That is an unbiblical doctrine of the Roman Catholic Church teaching that men and women must suffer in a place of torment to purge them of the sins of this life that is wholly and completely without biblical foundation. For this reason, Roman Catholics encourage those remaining in this world to pray for the deceased and thus enable their more rapid deliverance from torment. There is no need to pray for the dead, since those in hell cannot change their eternal condition and those in heaven would not; believers who have died are in the eternal bliss of paradise awaiting the resurrection day when they will be raised imperishable (1 Cor. 15:52).

## *The Doctrine of Glorification*

Paul wrote:

We know that all things work together for the good of those who love God: those who are called according to His purpose. For those He foreknew He also predestined to be conformed to the image

of His Son, so that He would be the firstborn
among many brothers. And those He predestined,
He also called; and those He called, He also
justified; and those He justified, He also glorified.
(Rom. 8:28–30)

The final step in this golden chain of events (predestination, calling, justification, glorification) describing God's
work of salvation in our lives is glorification. At Christ's
return, He will raise from the dead all who have died and
give them, as well as to believers who are still alive, perfect
resurrection bodies (Rom. 8:23; 1 Cor. 15:12–58). R. C.
Sproul wrote of the perfection that our future glorification
will bring about: "God will make all things right and keep
it that way throughout all eternity."[17]

## *The Doctrine of the Church*

This is a crucial doctrine for today, especially in global
missions. Some have operated under the erroneous notion
that a church is simply the fellowship of a few believers, as
if Jesus had said, "Wherever two or more are gathered in
My name, there is My church," which He did not say. It is
vitally important to understand what the Bible says about
churches, who the leaders should be, and what churches
are to do. The well-intended but naïve notion that a church
is simply a gathering of a few believers in Jesus' name

---

[17] R. C. Sproul, *Essential Truths of the Christian Faith* (Carol
Stream, IL: Tyndale, 1992), 211.

has resulted in much syncretism, heresy, carnal leadership, and spiritual manipulation. In the New Testament, a church can refer to a small house church, all the believers in a city, the churches in a region, or even the entirety of Christians throughout the world (Rom. 16:5; 1 Cor. 1:2; 16:19; 2 Cor. 1:1; 1 Thess. 1:1; Acts 9:31; Eph. 5:25; 1 Cor. 12:28). Additionally, a church planter's understanding of what a church is will drive the methodology he uses to plant churches and the objectives he has for them.

## What Is a Church

A church is not defined by the kind of building in which it meets, a specific number of members, the clothes they wear, or the kind of music they sing. A church is the body of "called out ones," from the word *ekklesia,* which is the etymological origin of the word *ecclesiastic.* The church is a body of believers, each of whom has a function, or role to play, according to the distribution of the gifts that the Holy Spirit has given, and Christ is the Head of this body.

The definition of *church* is most simply one that practices the three marks of a true church. Historically these three marks are the preaching of the Word, the ordinances of the Lord's Supper and baptism, and church discipline. Missiologists have sought to provide a fuller understanding for practical ministry. For instance, the International Mission Board has provided a very helpful definition of a church as follows:

1. A church is intentional about being a church. Members think of themselves as a church. They are committed to one another and to God (associated by covenant) in pursuing all that Scripture requires of a church.

2. A church has an identifiable membership of baptized believers in Jesus Christ.

3. A church practices the baptism of believers only by immersing them in water.

4. A church observes the Lord's Supper on a regular basis.

5. Under the authority of the local church and its leadership, members may be assigned to carry out the ordinances.

6. A church submits to the inerrant Word of God as the ultimate authority for all that it believes and does.

7. A church meets regularly for worship, prayer, the study of God's Word, and fellowship. Members of the church minister to one another's needs, hold each other accountable, and exercise church discipline as needed. Members encourage one another and build each other up in holiness, maturity in Christ, and love.

8. A church embraces its responsibility to fulfill the Great Commission, both locally and globally, from the beginning of its existence as a church.

9. A church is autonomous and self-governing under the lordship of Jesus Christ and the authority of His Word.

10. A church has identifiable leaders, who are scrutinized and set apart according to the qualifications set forth in Scripture. A church recognizes two biblical offices of church leadership: pastors/elders/overseers and deacons. While both men and women are gifted for service in the church, the office of pastor/elder/overseer is limited to men as qualified by Scripture.[18]

Mark Dever has emphasized marks of a *healthy* church. It should be noted that no one is saying that all of these are necessary for a gathering to be a church, but simply that a healthy church should be able to count these marks among its qualities. Notice also that each mark tends to grow directly from the mark before it and lead logically into the one that follows it.

1. Expository Preaching
2. Biblical Theology
3. Biblical Understanding of the Gospel
4. Biblical Understanding of Conversion
5. Biblical Understanding of Evangelism
6. Biblical Understanding of Church Membership

---

[18] International Mission Board, "Definition of a Church," January 25, 2005, http://imb.org/mobile/updates/storyview.aspx?StoryID=3838.

7. Biblical Church Discipline
8. Concern for Promoting Christian Discipleship and Growth
9. Biblical Church Leadership

## THE VISIBLE AND INVISIBLE CHURCH

The visible church is the church as we see it in the world. Some have referred to this as the church militant because we continue in the strife of spiritual warfare on this side of heaven's gates, with the church triumphant being those already in heaven. The invisible church is the church as God sees it and includes all believers in all of time (Eph. 1:22–23). The purity of the church refers to the degree of sanctification, freedom from sin, faithful obedience, and conformity to God's desires for His church. The seven letters to the churches in Asia Minor in Revelation 2–3 reveal the character of many churches in John's day, as well as many today, along with Christ's admonitions.

## THE MISSION OF THE CHURCH

The mission of the church has been debated at length for many years.[19] Differences of opinion range in degrees between proclamation of the gospel and ministry to the

---

[19] John Stott, *The Mission of the Church in the Modern World* (Downers Grove, IL: InterVarsity Press, 2015); David J. Hesselgrave, *Paradigms in Conflict: 10 Key Questions in Christian Missions Today* (Grand Rapids, MI: Kregel Academic and Professions, 2005); and Kevin DeYoung and Greg Gilbert, *What Is the Mission of the Church?: Making Sense of Social*

hurting. Wayne Grudem lists the primary purposes of the church as ministry to God through worship (Eph. 1:12; Col. 3:16), in the nurturing of believers (Col. 1:28), and to the world in missions and evangelism (Matt. 28:19–20; Acts 1:8; 11:29; 2 Cor. 8:4; Gal. 2:10; James 1:27; 1 John 3:17).[20] The church and her members are engaged in many different kinds of ministries around the world today. Some of the activities of the church are good things to do to minister to hurting people, but the primary goal is to know God and make Him known. Whatever else a church or ministry may do, if it is not adding the proclamation of the gospel to it, it is simply something that is good to do but not the mission of the church.

Some have considered biblical exhortations and examples of activities, responsibilities, ministries, and duties of churches as *means of grace*. This term is not to intimate that there is a mechanical conferring of salvation by rote or surface participation in the activity; rather, these are ways that more grace is received or realized by believers who genuinely practice them as a part of worship. Grudem lists them as teaching of the Word, baptism, the Lord's Supper, praying for each other, worship, church discipline, giving, exercise of spiritual gifts, fellowship, evangelism, and personal ministry to others.[21]

---

*Justice, Shalom, and the Great Commission* (Wheaton, IL: Crossway, 2011).

[20] Grudem, *Christian Beliefs*, 116–17.

[21] Grudem, *Systematic Theology*, 951.

## THE OFFICERS OF THE CHURCH AND THE PLURALITY OF ELDERS

As noted in the IMB definition of a church, the biblical officers of the church are pastors, or elders, and deacons:

> A church has identifiable leaders, who are scrutinized and set apart according to the qualifications set forth in Scripture. A church recognizes two biblical offices of church leadership: pastors/elders/overseers and deacons. While both men and women are gifted for service in the church, the office of pastor/elder/overseer is limited to men as qualified by Scripture.

Paul gives the church the qualification of these men in 1 Timothy 3:1–7 and Titus 1:5–9.

## *The Doctrine of Eschatology*

Eschatology refers to the study of last things. The Bible teaches that Christ will return bodily, suddenly, and in a way that will be visible to all (Matt. 24:44; Luke 17:22–24), yet we do not know the exact day when that will be. It is impossible for anyone to pinpoint the day (Matt. 24:36; 25:13; Mark 13:32). Jesus did teach that there would be signs of the end of the world that we could watch for, but the fact that many of these seem to have occurred through-out history still leaves many wondering about when that might be (Luke 21:28). Some believe that signs remain to be fulfilled so that He cannot return until the church has accomplished them, such as the preaching of the gospel to every people group, as we understand them. However, this would mean that the apostles who considered His return imminent were mistaken and He now still depends upon us for our obedience before He can culminate history, which seems to contradict His teaching that the Father already knows the day (Mark 13:32).

What we know for sure is that He *will* return and that there will be a resurrection and a day of judgment (Acts 1:11; 1 Thess. 4:16; Heb. 9:28; 2 Pet. 3:10; 1 John 3:2). It is difficult to become dogmatic about many of the details beyond this, although many insist on doing so. The reason for the debates about end times revolves around the millennial reign of Christ; *millennium* means "one thousand years."

Most of the controversy hinges upon the diverse interpretations of Revelation 20. While we do not want to needlessly plunge into the swirl of these debates or the minutiae of the arguments, the fact is that many of you have heard about these opinions with straw-men arguments and unfair assessments. Therefore, a quick review of the positions is warranted. The myriad of views including differing pre-, mid-, and post-tribulational views, historic, and dispensational millennial positions are not introduced here. These are simply the most basic ideas for a fundamental awareness of the terms.

## Millennial Views

Before continuing, take a moment to read Revelation 20:1–6. Before basing too many opinions on the actual verses in this passage, remember that the book of the Revelation is apocalyptic literature, which means that it is a revealing of a mystery, or something that has been hidden, is prophetic, and is by genre definition highly symbolic. In fact, George E. Ladd wrote, "In the apocalypses symbolism becomes the main stock in trade." Such symbolism is seen from the very first chapter when Jesus reveals to John the interpretation of the vision of One like the Son of Man walking among the seven golden candlesticks with the seven stars in His right hand and a double-edged sword coming out of His mouth (Rev. 1:20).

Moreover, the symbolism of numbers is repeatedly seen in the Bible, where numbers may not necessarily be literal. The number one thousand is not always to be understood literally. Psalm 50:10 says that the Lord does not need their sacrifices and offerings because the cattle on a thousand hills belong to Him. This is of course symbolic of all the cattle on every hill, not just those on a thousand hills. Peter wrote, "With the Lord one day is like a thousand years, and a thousand years like one day" (2 Pet. 3:8). This is also symbolic and is not teaching that only two days have passed by in heaven since the crucifixion of Christ. Even in a highly symbolic book, and being fully aware of biblical numerology, some have actually made their millennial view a litmus test for Christian fellowship.

These are important matters and an honest synthesis of all the passages related to them have led godly men and women to land at different places. Each of the positions has biblical warrant. Scholars who love the Lord with all their hearts have held the position that made the most sense to them, and some have switched from one position to another as their understanding of the arguments changed. There have been committed Christians throughout the history of the church holding to one or the other of these three positions. What are the basic understandings of these terms?

*Amillennial:* This position holds that there is no literal period of a thousand years and no future reign to come. Rather, any reign referred to is currently being realized, not coming in the future, and not a thousand literal years. Those of this position hold to the interpretation that when Christ returns there will be one resurrection, that of both the redeemed and the damned for the judgment, after which believers will live forever in the new heavens and the new earth.

*Premillennial:* The premillennial view holds that Christ will return suddenly and inaugurate a reign of a literal thousand years. Some within this position hold to two resurrections, one of the righteous and the second of unbelievers for judgment after a thousand-year earthly reign of Christ and believers, with Satan bound. Additionally, some variations of the premillennial position hold to two returns of Christ, the first being a secret one for believers and a second one seven years later that raises unbelievers for the judgment. Many believe that the rapture of the church will occur before the time of the great tribulation, and later Christ will return to the earth with the redeemed to reign with Him during a thousand-year reign.

*Postmillennial:* This position holds that Christ will return after the millennium, which will have been a period during which the church grew and advanced in number and influence. This position believes that the church will enjoy increased peace and the spread of righteousness throughout the world. This position is held by many as a fulfillment of Christ's parable of the kingdom comparison to a mustard seed that grows and becomes a large tree, or to the yeast that leavens a whole mass of dough. This position teaches that there will be one return of Christ and one resurrection, which will be for both believers and unbelievers.

## The Doctrine of Final Judgment

There will be a final judgment of everyone, believer and unbeliever, at the great white throne at the end of history (Rev. 20:11–15). The Lord Jesus will be the Judge (Acts 10:42; 2 Tim. 4:1; Matt. 25:31–33), and everyone will be judged according to what they have done (2 Cor. 5:10; Heb. 9:27; Rev. 20:12). Even believers will be called upon to give an account (Rom. 14:10–12). Yet believers

have the hope of God's promise that they will not be con-
demned when brought to this trial (John 5:24; Rom. 8:1).

## The Doctrine of Hell

Hell is a place of eternal torment and punishment. The
Bible describes it with terms that some interpret as literal
and others as symbolic: outer darkness, fire and brim-
stone, a lake of fire, a bottomless pit, weeping and gnash-
ing of teeth, devouring worms, and no rest or relief, day
or night, forever (Matt. 25:41; Mark 9:48; Luke 16:28;
Rev. 14:10–11; 20:14; 21:8). Although some believe that
the devil is the ruler of hell, the Bible teaches that hell was
prepared for the torture of him and the fallen angels, his
demons (Matt. 25:41; 2 Pet. 2:4; Rev. 20:14). This is the
eternal destiny for all who die without being born again
through repentance and faith in Christ.

## The Doctrine of Heaven

Heaven is the eternal home of God and the place where
He makes His presence most fully known, where saints
will enter upon death (Matt. 6:9; 25:34; Luke 23:43; 1 Pet.
3:22). It is where Jesus has gone to prepare a place for
each believer (John 14:3; 1 Pet. 3:22). The Bible speaks
of new heavens and a new earth that will be the eternal
home of believers when they leave this world (Isa. 65:17;
66:22; 2 Pet. 3:13). This restoration or renewal of the new
heavens and the new earth will be what the world would
have been like without the fall (Gen. 1:31), where everyone

knows and worships Him, where there is no sin, sickness, or death (Rom. 8:21; Rev. 21:1–4).

## The Hands: Shepherding God's Flock

> Therefore, as a fellow elder and witness to the
> sufferings of the Messiah and also a participant in
> the glory about to be revealed, I exhort the elders
> among you: Shepherd God's flock among you, not
> overseeing out of compulsion but freely, according
> to God's will; not for the money but eagerly;
> not lording it over those entrusted to you, but
> being examples to the flock. And when the chief
> Shepherd appears, you will receive the unfading
> crown of glory. (1 Pet. 5:1–5)

Most of you are either leading God's people now or are preparing to be able to do so. What is it to lead God's people? What does the Bible have to say about shepherds and shepherding?

The practical hands knowledge in this module focuses on shepherding God's flock. This emphasis is increasingly necessary around the world because of the genuine lack of biblical models and also because of the intentional spiritual manipulation and abuse by charlatans of the health and wealth heresies and cults. Unfortunately, even some evangelical missionaries think that power is the path for a leader to attain quick results and get others to do their will. We have examples to learn from and clear instruction in God's Word. Throughout the Bible, the various bodies of God's people always had someone providing leadership, such as prophets, priests, judges, kings, shepherds, apostles, or elders. What does the Bible teach about who is to shepherd, what shepherds should be, and whose flock it is that we are to shepherd?

## *Who Is to Shepherd?*

As we covered above, the biblical officers of a New Testament church are pastors or elders and deacons. We have already considered the call that is necessary to serve as pastor and the kinds of men they should be as we reviewed the guidelines Paul laid down in 1 Timothy 3:1–7 and Titus 1:5–9. But beyond their call and character, what are they specifically to do? What do we mean by the phrase "shepherding God's flock"?

This question is important because many assume that the leadership styles that are so effective in contemporary business models may be seamlessly incorporated and employed when shepherding the church. While there is much to learn from effective models of leadership, from both the world of politics and efficient management techniques for business, these are not to be imported wholesale into the church and mimicked by ministers for shepherding God's flock.

But there are some effective aspects of leadership from the business world that pastors would be wise to remember and practice. For instance, leadership specialists increasingly endorse and promote models of servant leadership, honesty, humility, and affirmation of others. In addition to these considerations, sound financial decisions from pastors require basic knowledge of budgets and accounting. Even marketing skills that emphasize research and contextualization to one's target area can serve the pastor as he seeks to know his church neighborhood and maintain awareness of changes so as to make wise decisions.

When God calls a man to ministry, we can say without a doubt that He has also called him to holiness, and this should color his leadership at every level. However, God has also called him to personal preparation for ministry. A call to serve assumes a call to prepare in every way available to him. This may mean learning about basic leadership and management skills, but above all else he must know and do what the Bible requires of shepherds.

As we prepare to serve our churches faithfully, we must know what the Bible says about that task. Some of you may live in cultures where the gospel has only recently penetrated and churches are still few and new. There may be no models for you to follow or older pastors who can mentor you, and so you may wonder, *What is a pastor to be, say, and do?* Others of you will have only known pastoral ministry models that are less than healthy. For instance, in one region of Andean South America, it was not uncommon for pastors of older established churches to discourage the planting of more churches or the facilitating of pastoral training for young men. Investigation revealed

that this was because they saw new churches and younger
trained pastors as a threat to their job security. Many of
them found comfort in being the "only game in town."
The only way around this challenge was to train younger
men and teach them what the Bible says about planting
churches and shepherding God's flock.

## *What Is a Shepherd to Do?*

The New Testament describes the leader of God's people as a pastor. He is also referred to as a servant, steward
of the gospel, overseer, shepherd, elder, minister, preacher,
pastor, counselor, leader, teacher, reconciler, prayer, evangelist, protector, provider, preparer, and pattern. That seems
like a pretty heavy job description, and in fact it is. The
Bible is quick to say that no one should aspire to the pastoral task lightly and without God's blessing, and chal-
lenges churches not to be hasty in the laying on of hands.
Men who aspire to pastoral ministry should be thoroughly
examined and held to the highest standards. This is to their
advantage since teachers will receive a greater judgment
than others. Let's examine some of these labels and roles
given to pastors and prepare our students to understand
their high calling and the demanding task to which God
has called them.

My children were very young when I was serving in
my first pastorate. They learned about church from the
unenviable position of being the pastor's kids. But the
sometimes unfairly high standards to which they were held

were often balanced out by kindness from church members simply because they *were* the pastor's children. After an evening service I was walking out of the sanctuary holding my three-year-old daughter's hand. She looked up at me and said, "Daddy, you're the boss of this church!" I turned red as I realized that several of the members heard her say this and were waiting to hear what my response would be. I winked at them and corrected her by saying, "No, sweetie, everyone here is my boss." Of course, neither of us was correct, but these two opinions of the role of a pastor represent two commonly held misconceptions. What does the Bible say?

## SERVE

A pastor is to shepherd the church by being a servant. Paul referred to himself and Timothy as slaves of Jesus Christ. That willing, life-long service to Christ is the pattern we are to emulate. Although we are to serve others as ministers and follow the example of Jesus who came to serve and not to be served, the pastor is not to be every member's smiling lackey or yes-man. We are to lead by serving our Lord as an example for others to follow. This means that we must serve them humbly, but keeping in mind that humility and humiliation are not synonymous (Phil. 1:1; 1 Cor. 4:1; Rom. 14:7–12; 15:17–18).

## STEWARD

Shepherds are also stewards of the gospel. God has entrusted the gospel message to His church and to pastors as faithful stewards who are to maintain its purity and spread its message throughout the world. As in the parable of the talents, faithful stewards of the gospel are to employ it wisely in order to maximize return on investment. To do this, shepherds must remain pure themselves, keep the message of the gospel pure, and be busy about the work of the gospel until Christ returns. Of course, to be found faithful in carrying out this aspect of gospel stewardship, one must know the difference between the pure gospel and one that has been mixed with worldly teaching. Toward that end we never stop learning, seeking the illumination of the indwelling Holy Spirit and measuring all teaching by the revealed Word of God like good Bereans (Acts 17:11; 1 Cor. 4:1–3; 1 Tim. 1:3–5, 11; 6:20–21; 2 Tim. 1:13–14).

In the Greek New Testament there are three primary words that speak of the role of pastor: *episkopos, poimen,* and *presbuteros.* The word *episkopos* is sometimes translated "overseer" or "bishop." The word is a compound of a prefix meaning "upon" and the word for "scope." The idea is that the person who is the *episkopos* is examining, guarding, watching, and even scrutinizing. He wants to keep the flock safe and pure. The word *poimen* is best translated "pastor" or "shepherd" and includes all the tasks that a shepherd would fulfill in caring for his flock, such as guiding, feeding, providing, and protecting. The third word is *presbuteros*, and it refers specifically to an elder. This may refer to a rank or to the senior age of the person with the title. The primary idea in ecclesiastical use derives from the wisdom that comes with age coupled with sound biblical teaching to guide and govern in the church. These are not three New Testament Greek words describing three different offices but like facets of a single gem are different ways of considering the office, role, and responsibility of a pastor.

## TEACH

Paul listed pastor-teacher among the types of leaders that God gave to the early church. "And He personally gave some to be apostles, some prophets, some evangelists, some pastors and teachers" (Eph. 4:11). Paul repeatedly stresses that the role of the pastor must include teaching. He states in the qualifications of pastors that they be apt to teach. He reminds Titus that the reason for this is so that they may proclaim sound teaching and refute bad doctrine. Paul wrote to ensure that his disciples encourage this aspect in their ministries also (1 Tim. 4:6–8, 11, 13–16; 2 Tim. 2:2; 3:14–17; 4:2; Titus 2:1). It is interesting to note that the purpose of a pastor-teacher was to prepare God's people for the work of the ministry, not to do all the work of ministry himself. Some mistakenly believe that the pastor is to do all of the work of ministry, including evangelizing, visiting, counseling, and teaching; but the Bible is

clear that a pastor-teacher is to prepare the body of Christ
so that each one may fulfill their own calling, having the
necessary training to do what God has called them to do.

When the early church recognized the need for servants to carry out the daily tasks of ministry responsibilities, they set aside the first *deacons*, a word that literally
meant "attendant, table waiter, or one who performed
menial tasks." The need arose in Acts 6 because the number of believers was multiplying, and these new believers
needed to be discipled. But the routine, daily tasks such
as the fair distribution of food to needy widows among
them, was becoming overwhelming. The apostles called the
people together and instructed them to name some men
to serve the tables so that they could give themselves to
the ministry of the Word of God and prayer: to preaching,
teaching, and pastoring. As a result of this decision and the
appointment of these deacons, the "preaching about God
flourished, the number of disciples in Jerusalem multiplied
greatly, and a large group of priests became obedient to the
faith" (Acts 6:1–7).

## What Is a Shepherd to Be?

God's Word clearly teaches that each one is to be faithful in the tasks specific to the role they are to play. It also
teaches that the pastor is not there to perform all of the
practical ministries of the church. However, while the pastor is not to "do it all," neither is he to lord his position
over the church members as an egotistical boss or supreme

commander. What then should a pastor be and do in order to biblically shepherd God's flock?

## PREACHER

Paul called himself a herald and a teacher (2 Tim. 1:11). The pastor must teach and preach the Bible, explaining it in such a way that unbelievers may hear the gospel, and God's people can grow through a balanced diet of the whole counsel of the Word of God. Assisting the hearers to understand and apply the truth of the Bible to their lives is a key role of the pastor-preacher. Proclaiming and explaining the Bible is a primary task of the shepherd. He should also serve as an evangelist, preaching the good news to the lost and hopeless. Yet, the preacher should not make every sermon an exclusively evangelistic one, as the flock must be fed and nurtured on the entire Word. However, the preacher must never forget that some of those in the congregation only pretend to be believers and actually still need to hear the gospel. Others sincerely believe that they are Christians, but often in the hearing of an evangelistic sermon they come to realize that they are not. The pastor must be discerning so as to balance his sermon mix to both feed the flock and to share the gospel's good news. The pastor must never forget his role as ambassador of Christ (2 Cor. 5:20), and as ambassador he is not allowed to change the message, only to deliver it faithfully as it was entrusted.

PASTOR

When Jesus restored Peter by the Sea of Galilee, He charged him to feed His sheep and shepherd the flock (John 21:16). Pastoring or shepherding includes counseling, rebuking, instructing, encouraging, marrying, burying, visiting, reconciling, leading and managing administrative affairs, training God's people, evangelizing, praying, and providing hospitality (1 Pet. 5:1–4).

PROTECTOR

One of the greatest blessings that God gives new believers is godly men who will shepherd them faithfully. Pastors are to protect the church from error and attack (Jer. 3:15). God calls pastors to be on guard and serve as overseers, remembering that He purchased the flock with blood (Acts 20:28).

PROVIDER

The pastor is also to serve as a provider, one who feeds the flock with the Bread of life (John 6:35; Matt. 4:4). In much the same way that Moses was used by God to provide manna for His people in the wilderness, the pastor is to be God's man providing the spiritual sustenance that the Bible nurtures us with today. Jesus reminded the devil during His temptations that man does not live on bread alone, and we thus realize that while the pastor is not to provide the physical food that we need, he is to feed the flock with the Word (2 Tim. 2:2).

PATTERN

The shepherd should guide the flock by being a model of the Christian life lived out. He is to seek to be what Christ would be if Christ were living His life through him (1 Tim. 5:17; 2 Tim. 1:13; Phil. 4:9). Of course, no human living among us today can fully meet this goal, but pastors aspire to live in a way that is in harmony with the messages they preach. Indeed, such dedicated desire to be what Christ desires will be noticed, and that in itself can serve as a model for others to imitate.

Borrowing from Eusebius's threefold office of Christ as prophet, priest, and king, we may similarly speak of the work of the pastor. A prophet speaks on God's behalf. In the Old Testament, one of the marks of a prophet was accurately foretelling the future, which does not happen today. But it is also true that the prophet was to forth-tell the Word of God, that is, to proclaim the Word of God, and it is in this sense that we may refer to the pastor as a prophet. He is speaking on God's behalf and declaring His word to His people. The pastor is also a priest in the sense that a priest is one who represents the people to God, interceding for them in prayer. Finally, the office of king refers to one who provides order and rule for the people of God but is always under the lordship of God Himself. The pastor as prophet, priest, and king seeks to speak to the flock on God's behalf as he proclaims His Word, serve them as priest as he intercedes for the flock and leads them to make proper sacrifice (Rom. 12:1), and provide order through the guidelines and parameters of the Word of God.

## Who Is the Flock?

The Bible gives us a number of metaphors to facilitate clear understanding of what the church is to be: the bride of Christ (Eph. 5:25–27; Rev. 19:7); the body (Eph. 1:22–23; 4:12, 15–16; Col. 2:19); a temple (1 Pet. 2:4–8); a holy priesthood (1 Pet. 2:5); a field (1 Cor. 3:6–9); a building (1 Cor. 3:9–10; Eph. 2:19–22); and God's flock (Pss. 68:10; 77:20; Isa. 40:11) in addition to others.

The flock of God was a metaphor easily understood by the first hearers and readers of the Old and New Testaments. The role of a shepherd caring for a flock made sense to them since it was a natural part of everyday life. The term also fit because a flock of sheep's inability to guide itself, provide food and water for itself, or defend itself was well known, making this an effective metaphor for many to understand (Jer. 23:1–4; 1 Pet. 5:2).

## What Should the Shepherd Guide Them to Do?

The primary activities of a local church are worship, evangelism, discipleship, prayer, fellowship, ministry, and missions. There is overlap between and among these, but the point here is not to definitively or exhaustively state the work of the church in the world today. Rather, we want to identify some of the kinds of ministries that shepherds are to lead a church in carrying out in biblically responsible ways.

## The Flock Is God's

Shepherds must always remember that the flock belongs to God. The church is not their own, even though the process of investing the whole of their lives to serve it may make that reality easy to forget. A pastor's zeal for the purity, health, protection, and edification of the local church can very easily become personal. In the Old Testament, Jacob, Moses, and David are all examples of men who shepherded the flock of another. While there is every reason to believe that they did so with as much energy and interest as if the flock had been their own, perhaps even more so, their faithful service of shepherding another's flock must be a model for pastors shepherding the flock of God.

Peter reminds shepherds that they are indeed to care for and pastor the flock in their charge, but to remember that they are merely undershepherds and that Christ is the Great Shepherd of the sheep (1 Pet. 5:1–4). A passage that underscores this idea is seen in Ezekiel, where God states that He will punish wicked shepherds and shepherd His flock Himself (Ezek. 34). The building up in knowledge and increase in numbers of the flock is certainly our prayer and desire, but it is God's doing, never a product of our own efforts. Christ said, "*I* will build My church" (Matt. 16:18, emphasis added). Jesus assures us that as the Good

Shepherd, He knows His sheep (Ps. 23; John 10:11, 14, 27).

A key passage for shepherds to keep in mind regarding their role in pastoring churches is the vision that John received in Revelation 1:12–20. In this vision he saw One like the Son of Man walking among seven golden lampstands, holding seven stars in His right hand, and having a double-edged sword coming from His mouth. Jesus Himself explains to John that the vision signifies that He walks among the churches and holds the messengers (pastors) in His hand; the sword represents the Word of God. This teaches shepherds that Christ is present among them, and they may trust in this promise (Deut. 31:8; Matt. 28:20). Pastors also have the great comfort that they are secure in His hand. While the devil and all the forces arrayed against the church and her pastors in this world may war against them and seek to remove or destroy them, Christ holds them securely. Since these things are true, we rest in the knowledge that Christ can care for His shepherds and the flocks they serve. He can remove unfit pastors or bless the committed ones because He is among them and holds them in His powerful right hand. Shepherds would do well to remember the Word of God to them through Peter:

> Shepherd God's flock among you, not overseeing
> out of compulsion but freely, according to God's
> will; not for the money but eagerly; not lording it
> over those entrusted to you, but being examples to

the flock. And when the chief Shepherd appears, you will receive the unfading crown of glory. (1 Pet. 5:2–4)

## My Prayer for You

*Father, I thank You for the disciples who are learning from this training material. I thank You that growth in being, knowing, and doing Your will is their desire. Bless them with Your divine protection in daily life and ministry. May they be clothed in Your armor, having their feet shod with the gospel of peace, wearing the belt of truth, having hearts covered with the breastplate of righteousness, and protected by the helmet of salvation. May they take up the shield of faith and rightly wield the sword of the Spirit, which is Your Word. Dear Lord, hold them in Your hand of favor and surround them with Your faithfulness. May they rest in Your grace, mercy, and forgiveness.*

*Fill them with the power of Your Holy Spirit. Hide them in Your presence, in Your secret place, in the hollow of Your hands, in the shadow of the Almighty, and in the shelter of Your wing. Protect them from the strife of tongues, from conspiracies, attacks, plots, rumor, slander, gossip, shame, disgrace, scandal, schemes, ridicule, and intrigues of the evil one. Surround them with a hedge of thorns.*

*Lead them not into temptation but deliver them from the evil one and his demonic predators that would destroy them.*

*Grant and fuel their desire and ability to purify themselves from everything that defiles body and spirit, bringing holiness to completion in the fear of You. Let them not grieve, quench, or vex Your Holy Spirit, nor let presumptuous sins have dominion over them.*

*Bless their reputations for Christ's sake. Please don't let those who hope in You ever be put to shame because of them. Lead them in paths of righteousness for Your name's sake. Let others see You in them. Grant them self-control, a passion for purity, and a heart for holiness, looking daily unto You and not to men, mindful that Your mercies are new every morning. Wash them clean in the blood of Jesus and keep a clean wind blowing through their hearts. And in all the ways that they have failed You and wasted resources and opportunities, restore the years that the locusts have eaten.*

*Oh Father, I pray that You will so use them that the knowledge of You will cover the earth as the waters cover the sea. Be glorified in each of them and give them burning hearts and open doors to do all Your holy will for the glory of Your name and the expansion of Your kingdom.*

*In Jesus' name, amen.*

## Suggested Resources

Beardmore, Roger O. *Shepherding God's Flock*. Hinton, VA: Sprinkle Publications, 1988.

Berkhof, Louis. *Manual of Christian Doctrine*. Grand Rapids, MI: Eerdmans, 1979.

Elwell, Walter A., and David G. Benner. *Baker Encyclopedia of Theology*. Grand Rapids, MI: Baker, 1984.

Goldsworthy, Graeme. *The Goldsworthy Trilogy: (Gospel and Kingdom, Gospel and Wisdom, The Gospel in Revelation)*. Milton Keynes, England: Paternoster, 2001.

Grudem, Wayne. *Bible Doctrine: Essential Teachings of the Christian Faith*. Grand Rapids, MI: Zondervan, 1999.

———. *Christian Beliefs*. Grand Rapids, MI: Zondervan, 2005.

———. *Systematic Theology: An Introduction to Biblical Doctrine*. Grand Rapids, MI: Zondervan, 1994.

Helopoulos, Jason, and Ligon Duncan. *The New Pastor's Handbook: Help and Encouragement for the First Years of Ministry*. Grand Rapids, MI: Baker, 2015.

House, H. Wayne. *Charts of Christian Theology and Doctrine*. Grand Rapids, MI: Zondervan, 1992.

Jeffery, Peter. *Christian Handbook: A Straight Forward Guide to the Bible, Church History and Christian Doctrine*. Darlington: Evangelical Press of Wales, 1988.

MacArthur, John and Master's College Faculty. *Rediscovering Pastoral Ministry.* Nashville, TN: Thomas Nelson, 1995.

Sproul, R. C. *Essential Truths of the Christian Faith.* Carol Stream, IL: Tyndale, 1992.

Spurgeon, C. H. *Lectures to My Students.* Grand Rapids, MI: Zondervan, 1979.

Whitney, Donald S. *Spiritual Disciplines for the Christian Life.* Colorado Springs, CO: NavPress, 2014.